To Alistair and Anne

with the author's good wishes.

Ken Hastings

Dec 06

IN A RIGHT STATE

IN A RIGHT STATE

The Reflections of an Education Inspector

Kenneth Hastings

The Book Guild Ltd
Sussex, England

The Book Guild Ltd.
25 High Street,
Lewes, Sussex

First published 1998
© Kenneth Hastings, 1998

Set in Times
Typesetting by
SetSystems Ltd, Saffron Walden, Essex

Printed in Great Britain by
Antony Rowe Ltd.
Chippenham, Wiltshire

A catalogue record for this book is
available from the British Library

ISBN 1 85776 395 5

Dedicated to Christopher Howard
and to
Robert John Neal

CONTENTS

ACKNOWLEDGEMENTS

My first thanks are to Stephen Kelly, sports journalist, who initiated me into the proper use of a word processor. He ought to have warned me, as Groucho Marx once said, that 'writing is an extremely tough racket', and then there is the sweat of mastering the keyboard. Even so, I was making reasonable progress with two chapters written, when I stumbled upon Bruno Bettelheim's remark that if you write an autobiography you 'bind yourself to lying, to concealment, to flummery'. I had to look up 'flummery' in the dictionary, and I found it covered everything from deceit to rubbish. I nearly gave up.

However, various friends and associates told me not to worry, so I kept at it. With gratitude I now acknowledge the encouragement I received at various times from Richard Allday, Judith Bell, David Bradshaw, Roy Caslake, Alison Coates, Margery Gaskell, Pamela Howard, Professor Eric Midwinter, Rosamund Pomeyie, Peter Renton, Doctor Donald Ross.

My particular thanks go to my friend and former colleague, John Chugg, for exposing the defects of earlier drafts and persuading me to do better. I also record my gratitude to members of my family. Above all, my greatest debt is to my wife, Joyce, who patiently monitored and, lovingly as ever, urged me on.

K.H.

PROLOGUE

And to make an end is to make a beginning.
The end is where we start from.

T. S. Eliot – 'Little Gidding'

On an early Spring day in 1986 I had taken my leave of all my colleagues, many of whom wished they were going too. Privately I was not sure whether I was a casualty or a deserter, such was my deeply ingrained sense of service. Now I was also saying a final goodbye to the office staff in the Leeds government office which had been my base for nearly seven years. They had interpreted my illegible handwriting without complaint, turned my untidy notes into impeccably presented visit notes or inspectorial reports, and at times in fairly diplomatic tones made it clear that I was not the only inspector whose typing they had to see to, nor indeed was I the senior person in the office, merely one of the subalterns as it were. To this day I value dearly the revised edition of *The Oxford Dictionary of Quotations* which they gave me as a parting gift.

Now I was relinquishing my role as Her Majesty's Inspector, a role I had been proud to be appointed to 16 years earlier. I could not quite decide my dominant feeling as I drove home along the ring road, with little likelihood of an attack of road rage as I now had plenty of time. I felt a great relief, an intense fatigue, and a pang of regret. I seemed to have been waiting months for this day, and now I was not absolutely sure what was ahead. In the days that immediately followed there would be more and more time to reflect, and no more work-generating envelopes arriving on my doormat, no more demanding telephone calls at all hours.

Over recent years my colleagues and I had become more frustrated. Our originally agreed right to plan most of our own priorities had slowly been eroded, as we were more and more directed to carry out quick surveys or instant visits at someone's political behest. Our opportunities for considered opinion making were becoming fewer. The feeling being shared was that the whole of the civil service, of which we were a small part, was under attack, that liberally expressed opinions were not relevant, and that moderation was merely a form of weakness.

Even worse in our own special work was the problem that we were not being given the time for 'district work', that part of our employment that had historically required us to liaise with local education authorities, not just to enable us to feed information regularly to our own department but also to engage in constructive dialogue with senior officials of the authority. In our 'general work' too, which meant being a regular visitor to colleges and schools, we had already started to lose touch. In the final seven years of my service, nearly 200 senior administrative personnel in our government department had left their posts for one reason and another. The absolute nature of some of our received instructions, proscribing any discussion, had left us in a right state.

In the course of time I began to wonder what exactly my years in education had added up to. Had I achieved anything constructive? Had I merely been a self-important *fonction-naire*? Were the lessons I had learned of value in themselves? What on earth was happening in the education system? What will happen if the 'guardians' are pensioned off? It is easy with hindsight to say, 'I told you so', but the occurrence of so many dire situations in schools in the later 1990s would come as no surprise to all those who had originally served as Her Majesty's Inspector of Schools, nor equally to those who, like myself, belonged to the further and technical education group of inspectors within that organisation.

My anger did not quickly subside. Fortunately I now had the time to observe my friends and neighbours more closely, especially the small children. It pained me to think that such an interest today could be misconstrued, when all I was doing was to enjoy the sight of children at play, especially when they were taking risks or driving their parents mad. On more than one occasion I watched a small child run breathlessly up a huge mound of newly excavated soil on a building site near to my home. It was just the sort of challenging thing I would have done at his age, six or seven. He would turn skilfully at the exact point where his momentum petered out, and rush downhill, just retaining his balance. Each time I was waiting for him to sink up to his neck in soft soil. Each time he survived without any problem. Was this prophetic? Is there not hope of children being able to survive the perils of life? Do we all worry too much?

In the course of time I began to recall my own early days. What started off as innocent reflection became the subject matter of this book. The story became more than a story, a quest for meaning, a critique of the system, a search for the right things.

I must look again to T. S. Eliot:

> right action is freedom
> ....
> For most of us ... undefeated
> Because we have gone on trying;
> We, content at the last
> If our temporal reversion nourish
> The life of significant soil.

PART 1
A FIRE TO BE KINDLED

The mind of a child is not a vessel to be filled, but a fire to be kindled.

Confucius

There really was a time prior to the Second World War, when the power of the ordinary schoolteacher was unchallenged and most parents exerted on their children an influence that was firm and beneficial.

At the time I describe in chapters 1 to 3, teachers and parents shared a responsibility. It was not discussed; it was taken for granted. Children were conditioned to experience pleasure and pain, to find role models such as famous heroes and heroines, to develop a clear idea of right and wrong, and to know their future place in society. The mass media as we know them today did not exist; the daily papers were still restrained in their tone and format; and the wireless was not yet pervasive.

As the 1930s progressed, there was little real awareness of the shadow of war, especially among young children. The eventual 1939 to 1945 conflict merely strengthened our optimistic belief in the British way of life and our resolve to beat the foreigner. Despite the bloodshed and the destruction, there were continuing hopes that hard work and Christian faith might bring preferment in this life, if not in the life to come – especially for children who had won scholarships to attend the grammar school.

One's passage into adolescence during these years was inevitably affected by the prospect of military service. 'Who would true valour see?' and 'Fight the good fight' were sufficiently sung in school assemblies to prepare most young men and women in all true belief to be ready to die for their country. For most of the war years, technology had not yet shaped the massive weapons of destruction that are commonplace today. Despite the horrors to be perpetrated, grammar school boys managed to follow a traditional lesson timetable before they marched off to war.

Educational technology was just about at the magic lantern stage. The inspectorial standards of the 1990s, if they could have been applied, would have simply indicated the absence of visual aids, the emphasis on whole-class teaching, the reliance on rote-learning, the lack of an integrated curriculum, and the absence of clearly defined objectives – and of mission statements.

Yet, for countless young men and women such a schooling is remembered and still acknowledged as a first preparation for life's perils and pleasures.

1

Early Days

Even a child is known by his doings, whether his work be pure, and whether it be right.

Proverbs 20.11

Family folk tales persist, distorting real memory. Throughout my childhood I was so often told about how, as a crawling baby, I had chewed lumps of coal that I thought this was normal baby food. In the back streets of Gainsborough, on the northern border of Lincolnshire, where I was born in the 1920s, coal was readily available from the minefields of nearby Nottinghamshire and South Yorkshire, but only if you had enough money to pay the coalman. Somehow my parents managed to afford enough coal to heat the back boiler behind the kitchen fire and provide a modest supply of hot water. Being bathed in a shallow tin bath in front of the kitchen fire must have given tiny hands the chance to seek the chips of black stuff lying on the hearth rug, after the coal scuttle had been noisily discharged. I suspect that my alleged chewing of coal was more a substitute teething ring, not an early aptitude for mineralogy.

My family chroniclers were also fond of reminding me, in suitably grave tones, that at the age of two I was rushed off to hospital after a continuous earache that finally necessitated surgery to save my life. This, of course was another anecdote to make me cringe, but these were indeed hard times. The absence of antibiotics added to every parental trauma whenever children were ill, and the absence of a national health service meant that money had to be found to pay for the doctor's visit, or for a visit to a doctor's surgery, and for whatever foul-tasting medicines were dispensed. Ever sensitive to smells and sounds, I remember several visits to an awesome doctor in a tall, dimly lit Georgian building, where mysterious muted conversations accompanied the smell of ether and of standard medicaments. After such early experiences, I have always hated illness, and I pray to recover from any ailment as quickly as possible.

No health problems stopped me in my fifth year when I first went to the local infants school. Unlike some of today's children, I had experienced no pre-school or nursery group. In my family and in our town such luxuries were unknown. However, I was not averse to learning and went off happily on the first day. I discovered this huge expanse of hard-surfaced playground at the side of the school was an arena for assertive play. As the early Autumn mornings became cooler, I raced around excitedly, exhaling spurts of steam to demonstrate my transformation into one of those roaring trains that thundered over the railway bridge within yards of the school. It was at that formative time, too, that I was one day placed in disgrace in the corner of the classroom and severely admonished. Miss Nelson's red cardboard pointer was being waved unmistakably at my face. Even at this age I was not conforming, nor was I able to sustain attention once the message was menacing my very being. Yet I was not alone in trouble, and another malign spirit named Peter became my rival in classroom misdemeanours. We vented our spleen at the end of one school day by rushing out of school and on the way home tearing up the drawings entrusted to us for safe home delivery. We stuffed the pieces into a rain spout in the boundary wall of the nearby church, but with no cognizance at that age of the possible wrath of either Jehovah or Miss Nelson, or Mother and Father.

Pleasure and pain were becoming established in my consciousness. On one social occasion my joy in standing behind the conductor of the local works brass band was quickly reduced by the thunder of voices of reprimand and the firm, though not too malicious slap on the backside that rewarded my initiative. Much of my early learning was like this. Sometimes, the things that I was required to do, rather than the things that I instinctively wanted to do, could be quite daunting. The first time that I was to run alone to a general store near to home, I was instructed to purchase a bundle of wood and a packet of Lux soap powder, and 'don't lose the money'. I kept repeating the order to myself as I hurried along. The benevolent 'Open All Hours' storeman successfully unscrambled my order for a bundle of Lux and a packet of wood. Washday proceeded without a hitch.

The large tin washtub, the dolly, and the mangle with its huge wooden rollers were familiar furniture in the wash-room off the kitchen. My fascination with the rotation of the rollers and the grinding of the adjacent cogs was disturbed on one occasion by a shriek of pain from sister Muriel. She had, unbeknown to me, placed her hand in front of the rollers at the exact moment when I decided – in pursuit of more learning – to turn the handle. Someone else's pain in this case distracted from the question of who was to blame. Curiously, in that early environment of kitchen and washhouse, there was one particularly serious event whose significance was only in later years apparent to me. I saw Father one day, with some gravity, displaying a gold watch and chain, which I had never noticed before. Grandfather James Juniper had died. This was the inherit-ance. My own Father always preferred this watch, or over the years subsequent pocket watches, and wound them regularly to the day he died at the age of 86.

Much of significance in my life at this time happened outside the house. One Sunday in October 1930 a strange noise caused everyone to rush out of doors and look up at the sky. There we all saw this large, cigar-shaped airship

7

moving slowly and very visibly in the direction of the school. Michael Green, the author of *The Art of Coarse* books describes the same experience in 'The Boy Who Shot Down an Airship'. He too was a small boy at the time, and he suggests that one of his playmates up the road had shot at the airship with an air rifle, possibly damaging one of the gas bags. Whether that was of consequence or not, the R101 later that day crashed in France, killing most of its passengers and crew. None of this intelligence reached my young ears. My own intentions were not hostile. Indeed, the sight of this airborne vehicle brought a new dimension into my next playtime, but it was more difficult to be an airship than to be a train.

Like all small children I loved exercise and movement. Tumbling head over heels down a nearby grassy hill only five minutes away from the house, or racing around the narrow alleys at the back of our street kept me constantly active. I also aspired to drive everything on wheels, whether a toy scooter or a very primeval model of the go-cart. However, there was real excitement one day when I was taken for a long ride in a real car – an open tourer. This belonged to one of our wealthier lodgers, of whom there were many to supplement our domestic income. The experience of being driven to the Lincolnshire coast and back again broadened my repertoire of engine noises and driving antics. Evidence of my early driving ambition is to be found in the first of the photographs reproduced later in this book. Perhaps the uncertain expression arises from the lack of real movement and noise.

My desire for self-assertion, coupled with my imitative instincts, prompted me on one occasion to collect a bundle of old newspapers and carry them to the street corner. There, in as loud a voice as I could manage, I stood for some time shouting, 'NEWSWIERP! NEWSWIERP!' This vocal injunction stuck in my mind for years afterwards. I never knew whether I was saying '*News of the World*' or '*Gainsborough News*' or just mispronouncing 'newspapers'. Certainly I was copying some impressive street vendor who, unlike me, knew what he was on about. Lack of sales, or of any response whatever, quickly diminished my enthusiasm.

Mine was not an environment to make me really street-wise, and in those days playing in the street was a relatively safe and innocent affair. Despite misdemeanours and rebukes, I was eager to learn and full of curiosity, especially over things mechanical – an attribute unnoticed in my later education and relatively undeveloped, although to some extent fulfilled when I later in life became a Royal Engineer. Under the combined influence of home and school, I was coming to terms with words and numbers without difficulty. My abacus at home was the equivalent of today's electronic calculator, and I was constantly encouraged by Father to take my first arithmetical steps. In due course I took to reading with pleasure, and the competitive presence of sister Muriel and cousin Joyce, both of whom were a year or so older than myself, stimulated an early mastery of *Chick's Own Comic* and other infant publications. In addition, my tactile and manipulative skills were being partly expressed through frequent sessions with toy bricks of various shapes and sizes. My persistence, so I was told, was evident when I refused to go to bed until I had not only completed the tower of the day, but had also dismantled the edifice and returned each brick to its container in an exact fit.

Amid these early years of innocent play and gradual learning, only the occasional displeasure apart from illness intervened. Regular dental care for children of my generation was almost unheard of, so recourse to the dentist when a real need arose was bound to be painful. On one occasion the dentist was brought to our house, and I was persuaded by several adults to undergo a tooth extraction. The howls of pain and the spate of tears lasted only a short time. Other pleasanter distractions intervened.

In 1931, we all moved to the other end of the town. This enabled Father to be nearer to his new place of work. Having been made redundant as an Engineer's Clerk, he was fortunate to be taken on as a Clerical Officer in the Inland Revenue. The result for Muriel and myself was a move to another school, new friends to find, and new play areas to explore. These were times of unemployment, recession, and economic deprivation, but I had no idea or understanding of just how hard-up our parents had been. I was too young and innocent to know that not all children are loved, not all Fathers have a paid job, not all Mothers can afford to feed their families, not all householders own the house they live in – we did not own ours – nor does every household have paying lodgers to whom small boys and girls must be constantly polite. Equally I was unaware that not all parents provide toys and books, however modestly, nor encourage their children to learn and to heed the wisdom of their elders.

I had no idea either that other countries in the world were quite different from ours, or that the lives of millions of people could be affected by famine, pestilence or war.

But though I did not know it, I was learning to observe, to imitate, to imagine, to have fun and to compete. I was happy and cared for, and very ready for the next stage of my education and upbringing.

2

Developing Skills: In Search of a Scholarship

> I said ... how, and why, young children were
> sooner allured by love, than driven by beating, to
> attain good learning.

Roger Ascham, *The Schoolmaster* (1570), preface

Mr Smith, my first class teacher in the new school, was a
dapper little man. His trousers were perfectly creased, and
the top pocket of his jacket displayed a neat cohort of
pencils on either side of a large fountain pen. Father's
trousers were not so well pressed, and he had no fountain
pen. Now what really impressed me about Mr Smith was
that he wore highly polished SHOES. Father wore highly
polished BOOTS, just as his own father, James Juniper, had
done before him. Repeatedly I said to Father, 'I wish you
wore shoes like Mr Smith.' Father, who was a courteous,
patient man, continued to wear boots.

All the teachers in the school, including Mr Smith, were
in total command. Miss Larrett, the only lady teacher at
that time, was not outmatched by the men. With a sharp rap
over the knuckles from a large ruler, she completely discouraged all spelling mistakes; and her stern face quelled
any other aberration. Mr Proctor, a young but heavily built
man, was more than a match for any act of defiance. Mr
Little was an ace dispenser of the cane – three short
unconnected swishes led to one lethal blow that made the
middle fingers glow like red-hot coals. In contrast, Mr

11

Musgrove, managing the older boys, was a less repressive and more popular teacher. He successfully enlarged our grasp of tonic-solfa, and taught us quite a repertoire of traditional songs, ranging from 'The Raggle-Taggle Gypsies-O' to 'The Lincolnshire Poacher', with diversions into classic Scottish numbers such as 'Ye Banks and Braes o' Bonny Doon' and 'Caller Herrin''. 'The Lincolnshire Poacher' was one of my favourites. I hoped that one day I too might go poaching 'on a shiny night in the season of the year.' Of Mr Kenyon, the Headmaster, little was seen or heard, which probably meant he was doing his job very well. There were no regular assemblies over which he could preside, and this helped the class teacher to rule supreme.

Many years later I was told by Mother that she had actually spoken to Mr Kenyon from time to time. I am not sure how or where this communication took place, for it was almost unheard of for parents to talk to staff, except in emergencies. Somehow, despite the fact that I was reasonably fed and not unhappy, Mother had said she was worried because I was such a thin lad, especially in the legs. 'Look at race horses, Mrs Hastings,' replied Mr Kenyon. 'Look at race horses.'

What made the staff dedicated and industrious was that they were also the products of an elementary schooling. Since the last century this system had taught proficiency in the three R's – reading, writing, and arithmetic – and turned children into God-fearing individuals, fit for 'the useful work of life'. A certain severity in both discipline and curriculum was therefore natural. Only as the 1930s progressed were there signs from the Board of Education that elementary education should be viewed afresh. The onset of war in 1939, however, was largely to prevent any radical change, although a significant review of education was to take place during the war years, with the 1944 Education Act laying down the pattern of early post-war education. Meanwhile, in the mid-1930s, it did not occur to small boys like myself, whether fat or thin, that things at school could, or should, be different.

My contemporaries and I accepted our schooling quite happily. We never missed what we never had, and what many of today's primary school children and their parents take for granted. School meals were not provided; space and materials for art, music, or drama were very limited; there were no out-of-school clubs or activities; and no playing fields. At the end of the morning, children went home for 'dinner' and returned promptly for the afternoon lessons. The playground, as ever, brought a glorious release from the confinement of rigid desks and the formality of the learning process.

Back in the classroom, amid a relentless timetable, Scripture brought us all to order. Since the school was non-denominational, there was no sectarian bias, and the main purpose was to learn by heart and to recite in unison some of the best known passages in the Holy Bible. Most people of my generation who had this grounding can still quote a number of psalms, the Beatitudes, or the Ten Commandments. Learning by rote in this way at least gave children an awareness of language and a response to verbal rhythm that would remain with them forever. In all this learning and recitation, there was little or no overt explanation of what it all really meant. To my simple mind God remained a mysterious bearded figure, rather like a cross between Father Christmas and Grandfather James Juniper.

Literacy, encouraged through Scripture, was further stimulated through the constant practice of reading and writing, with plenty of attention to the basics. Punctuation was tackled through wrestling with unpunctuated excerpts of conversation from *Alice in Wonderland*. The most common parts of speech, such as nouns, verbs, adverbs and adjectives, were formally identified on the blackboard. Simple sentences were dissected to denote the subject and the predicate. All this was accepted as part of the normal diet, with little discomfort, swallowed if not digested. The happiest part of English after these basics was composition, and I remember with pleasure that I was once allowed to write at length throughout several lessons describing 'A Film I Have

Seen'. *Charlie Chan in Egypt* at one of our local picture-houses had so stimulated my imagination that I could hardly wait to describe the mystery and menace of some dirty work in the Pyramids, with Charlie Chan, the inscrutable Oriental detective, cracking yet another case after frightening forays into subterranean chambers and hitherto unopened tombs. Being allowed to write in this way with freedom and at my own pace was a refreshing experience. It was certainly a less rigid approach to the curriculum.

One activity that literally kept us on the straight and narrow was handwriting, which involved formal instruction and practice in shaping one's letters to the desirable norms. These were derived originally from the Civil Service and commercial practice, with appropriate form and slope. Many of the original highly ornate curves and lines had been modified to produce letters that could be copied and joined easily, so helping a child later to develop its own individual style. The letters reproduced on the opposite page are a fair example of those still being taught to children in the 1930s. My own handwriting went through several stages of size and slope at this stage, despite admonitions from the teacher, and later developed still more liberties.

The correct norms in terms of social behaviour were also touched upon, with English serving as a useful vehicle. I clearly remember having to write an imaginary letter to a relative to say thank you for a present received. As I did not receive many presents from relatives, I could only think of Aunt Edith, who had once given me a bar of chocolate. There was not a great deal for a child to say about receiving and eating a bar of chocolate, though I was not competent to put it so succinctly. In the end I thanked Aunt Edith 'for being very kind and giving me a tasty bar of chocolate, which I enjoyed very much. I hope you are well. Your loving nephew, Kenneth.' I purposely did not say that the chocolate was NICE, since this word was not allowed, and although I thought that APPETISING might be more suitable I was unsure of the spelling and unwilling to risk making a mistake. An added dimension to this exercise was

14

From *Teaching and Organisation*, edited by P. A. Barnett, Longmans, Green & Co. 1903

15

that we were given a real envelope to address, with particular attention to spacing and spelling. The envelope was then glued to the page, as a permanent example of how to do it, so it had to be right.

As I moved up the school, the arithmetic syllabus was relentlessly pursued. It covered the simple rules of addition, subtraction, multiplication, and division; in money, familiarity with pounds, shillings, and pence, not forgetting the halfpenny and the farthing; in weight and capacity, a knowledge of the basics; in vulgar fractions, an understanding of the simplest forms; and in decimals, multiplication by whole numbers and how to get the right number of places after the point. All essentials in measurement and volume were learned by rote, as were the multiplication tables. Mental arithmetic was an almost daily event. Having such constant drills in number relationships prepared us for the slightly more demanding problems to be worked on for the Grammar School Entrance Examination.

Of the other subjects on the timetable, apart from music already mentioned, my recollections are more limited. In art, I recall copying a rather stereotyped pastoral scene of green and yellow fields, unaware that my colour vision was imperfect, a deficiency that was to be detected only when I was undertaking military service many years later. I also rather enjoyed making paper book covers as another art activity, and coating the covers with a mixture of water paints and oil that produced a vivid, veined finish. A more energetic activity was physical training conducted in the playground. Later on, some semi-gymnastic exercises were performed in the central corridor, which was quite wide, and it was during one of these lessons that I managed to fall awkwardly over the vaulting horse, causing as much of a shock to the teacher as to myself. In considerable pain from a dislocated elbow, I was transported to that dreaded local surgery and, after a minimal administration of ether, was correctly re-formed.

A much more pleasant curricular highlight, firmly entrenched in my mind, was the day on which we actually

16

left the classroom, complete with notebooks and other minor equipment, and proceeded in well-behaved crocodiles to the nearby River Trent. There along the bank we assembled two simple tripods a hundred yards apart, measuring carefully with a Gunter's chain. We had previously been told nothing at all about Gunter, who in fact was an early astronomer and surveyor. Our first tripod had been erected opposite a large tree on the other bank of the river. Using large pins inserted into soft paper boards placed on top of each tripod, we made an alignment from the first tripod to the tree and also to the second tripod, marking these in pencil. A sighting from the second tripod back to the first tripod and then to the tree across the river produced more pencilled lines. Back in school, the two sets of lines were put together to produce one right-angled triangle, with a known base. Finally, by measurement on the scale used, we determined the width of the river. No mention at this stage of Pythagoras, nor any thought as to who would want to measure the width of a river, or why, or who were the first people to use such a method.

Even more exciting, not just because they were national events, but also because they meant whole days out of doors away from school, were the Silver Jubilee of King George V and Queen Mary in 1935, followed by the coronation of King George VI in 1937. Each important day was a celebration, for which we were taken in brightly bedecked horse-drawn drays to a large tract of land outside the town. There we had unlimited quantities of sandwiches, sweetmeats and soft drinks, and endless time to play without too much supervision. On each occasion, the children's ranks were obediently assembled in the late afternoon, and the return journey made without mishap. These events were paralleled up and down the country. One historian, G.A.N. Lowndes, records in *The Silent Social Revolution* that for the 1935 event there were thousands of children assembled in Hyde Park, London over a stretch of two miles of roadways and stands, and they left not a trace of paper. The park cleaners of the Office of Works found the park cleaner

17

at the end of the afternoon than it had been before the children arrived in the morning. So far as I can remember, the school children of Gainsborough were just as impeccably behaved. There were no litter louts in those days.

In the mid-1930s our annual family holiday was another much-anticipated event, because unlike so many of today's children we were not exposed from infancy to a regular range of public events, foreign travel, or journeys by car or train. Provided enough money had been saved, we travelled by steam train to Cleethorpes or Skegness and were lodged in a modest seaside boarding house for a week. One year for a change, but really because money was limited, we had a week of daily train trips to different destinations in Lincolnshire, thanks to the availability of ten-shillings-a-week tickets. On each day we took packages of home-made sandwiches, as it was not within the family budget to eat out. In any case, there was not a huge variety of cafeterias or restaurants. Self-sufficiency was the rule, but there was genuine enjoyment for free, whether in merely paddling in the sea or playing on the sands. The smell of the Grimsby fish docks through which the train passed en route to Cleethorpes was less of a pleasure. Nor was I particularly happy during the visit to Lincoln when taken to see the ancient dungeons of Lincoln Prison. The tour of the Cathedral later on was a relief.

Like most elementary school children, I was certainly impressionable. Thus, as our standard of living slowly improved, leading to more pocket money, visits to matinee performances at the local cinema were most formative. It was not long before I was imitating the antics of the Three Stooges, the exasperation of comedian Edgar Kennedy, or the posture of Tarzan. Boy Tarzan, of course, was more my style, and on one occasion, after seeing him running incessantly through the jungle, I rushed out of the cinema, through the market square and along the main road to home, totally transformed into my young hero. I arrived home, red-faced and triumphant, and instantly demolished a plate of sandwiches. On other occasions, I particularly enjoyed Gaumont British newsreels when, after the boring bits about someone called Mr Chamberlain or other bigwigs, they gave reports of important football or cricket matches, enabling me to see the experts at work.

By today's standards you could hardly say that my contemporaries and I were properly kitted out for our own games of sport. We had no special shirts or boots or equipment. Our games were played in the street or in nearby fields, where we could be left without any fear of molesters or abductors. School holidays were one long game. I remember keeping a pocket diary and diligently entering 'Played football with R.A., L.H., and J.C.', followed the next day by 'Played football with L.H., J.C., and G.N.', and so on. Our games were always played in small groups. I never played in a formal team game until several years later. When I was not with my friends, I was out in the street kicking a tennis ball against the front wall, and seriously scuffing my shoes.

My enthusiasm for cricket was slightly diminished after several unfortunate episodes that resulted in broken windows. On one occasion, I was struggling to master the art of delivering a googly ball. Not having a real cricket ball, I had purloined a large potato and whittled it down to size with a penknife. The first time I bowled towards a makeshift wicket near to the house, the potato flew too high and went straight through the living-room window. For this misdemeanour, apologies were of no use and a considerable loss of pocket money ensued. In my enthusiasm for the art of propulsion, whether with tennis ball, potato, or stone from a home-made catapult, I inadvertently began to crack more window panes. It was just my bad luck that we lived opposite the local 'bobby'. This, of course, meant speedy detection of my crimes, the first step being PC Cox's knock on our door followed by 'I think he's been at it again, Mrs H . . .' In time, I learned more accuracy and restraint, after much suffering. Throughout these years, any damage caused by myself or by friends with similar efforts was purely accidental. Vandalism in our neighbourhood was unheard of.

When I was safely contained indoors, I had plenty to occupy my time. The wireless provided interesting diversions for both adults and children. We marvelled at being able to hear a description of a cricket match, whether in London or at the bottom end of the globe. This was the time of Len Hutton and Don Bradman, batsmen supreme, and of Harold Larwood, the body-line bowler. There was a different pleasure for children whenever they listened to a special programme every Sunday on Radio Luxembourg. After various personal responses to individual Ovaltineys who had sent in their special requests, we were treated to a secret message dictated in Ovaltiney code by no less than THE CHIEF OVALTINEY. Each message was quickly decoded, encouraging us all to behave politely and to work hard. Listening children throughout the land then sang with great gusto:

> 'We are the Ovaltineys, little girls and boys.
> We wake each morning bright and gay,
> So we enjoy our work and play.
> We all love a song, a story.
> Won't you share our joys?
> At games and sports we're more than keen.
> No merrier children could be seen;
> Because we all drink OVALTINE
> We're happy girls and boys.'

How incredibly innocent compared with today's media messages to children! Yet in that era the Sunday rendezvous captured the imagination of thousands of youngsters. Many of them, now in their golden years, can still recite this song.

Voices, figures and concepts of authority seemed to pursue me throughout my childhood. Through attendance at Sunday School, reinforced by teaching at school, I knew that Jesus Christ had suffered persecution and was nailed to the cross. Unhappily for me, there was some confusion in my mind over the meaning of persecution. Unbeknown to my parents, I was in the habit of trespassing into a builder's yard, where baulks of timber and stacks of old railway sleepers were ideal for hide-and-seek with other children. We made our access by excavating a shallow depression under one of the fences, which were too dangerous to climb as they were formed of spiked iron bars. One day we saw that a large notice had been fixed to the fence: TRESPASS-ERS WILL BE PROSECUTED. I stopped with dread, at first reading this as PERSECUTED. If I was caught tres-passing, I would be NAILED TO THE CROSS like Jesus Christ. I was deterred from trespassing – for a short time at least.

Normally I did not confuse my prefixes, and reading skill was something encouraged at home, apart from school. Mother and Father in fact always stimulated our interests and knowledge. Leisure time at home was much more of a family occasion than today, with everyone joining in word games or puzzles, or with the children playing separately but within easy sight of the parents. Father frequently offered arithmetical problems from a thick book called *Clarke's Correspondence Course*. For example, 'If it takes 3 men 12 hours to dig a trench 120 yards long, how many men will be needed to dig a 200 yards trench in 10 hours?' I was too young to see the unstated assumption in this – no fatigue, no drunkenness, no bad weather, no derelictions of duty – dig your hearts out, workers! At other times I would lose myself happily in *Newnes' Pictorial Knowledge*, in seven illustrated volumes, covering everything from Ancient Civ-ilisations to Modern Times, a veritable mine of information which I used for years afterwards. Mother and Father must have saved for months to pay for it. It was worth every penny.

Music was also a formative influence in these years. Father, who was a self-taught pianist, played both from the score and by ear, with a very wide repertoire of excerpts from Schubert, Mendelssohn, Beethoven or Brahms, as well as popular songs from *Maid of the Mountains* or *Showboat*. Mother's forte was to buy a gramophone record whenever finances allowed – some records were bought at Woolworths

21

for 6d (sixpence) each. Added to our earlier collection, they gave us an extensive choice of military marches, piano, violin and orchestral music. My love of the violin, which I learned to play in adolescence none too well, dated from hearing records of the great maestro Fritz Kreisler. The wireless also added to our musical fare, as popular dance bands such as Jack Payne's and Henry Hall's, and orchestras like Geraldo's and those of the BBC became a regular part of home life.

I learned many years later that one of Father's uncles had been a concert pianist at the turn of the century. As for my own nearer relatives in the 1930s, I am not sure about their cultural talents, but one or two had skills that impressed me. Uncle Charlie, living in Bawtry, had plenty of mechanical skill. He rode a motorcycle, and for a time earned his living as a commercial photographer. He then took to repairing shoes for a living, and showed Mother how to put new soles on the family shoes. He also repaired a buckled front wheel on my bicycle after I had collided with a delivery van. I escaped injury, and the van was unimpaired. Other relatives I found harder to fathom, since they often had little to say. Secretly, however, I admired my laconic Uncle Tom, who came from Mother's village and always made me think he was up to something crafty. I was sure that he was the Lincolnshire Poacher, and I felt secretly pleased when Mother sometimes said I had the look of Uncle Tom about me.

Sadly, I can recall no pleasure from encounters with my most elderly relatives. One of my grandmothers lived in a terraced house, with her own mother – at the period I recall, they must have been in their seventies and nineties respectively. Their constant companion was an elderly spaniel, whose body odours made my nostrils twitch. I remember them all sitting by the kitchen fire in silence each time we visited. Their eventual departure from this life is a confused memory of drawn curtains and suppressed weeping. Then there were no more visits to that quiet terraced house.

Encounters with friends and neighbours at home were

much more interesting and rarely sorrowful. I was too immature to feel any compassion for a rather eccentric middle-aged gentleman who lived up the road with his mother. Regularly other boys and I would provoke him by spreading our collections of cigarette cards along his front garden wall. Before long, Mr B would appear like a genie, hurling abuse and ordering us to 'Get them mucky fag cards off my new wall!' Other near neighbours treated us as cordially as if we were their own children, especially a couple who had emigrated from Scotland. It took me a long time before I could understand their accent. In those days, children seldom came across strangers of any sort and were not exposed to the variety of accents one hears today in our highly mobile, multi-cultural society. Local communities were tightly knit, and friendships largely confined to one's own street.

These, then, were typical of the experiences shaping my life at this stage. Happy in my own boyish thoughts and activities, I was unaware that living standards were improving, society was becoming more mechanised, and public entertainment was becoming more popular, with 40 per cent of the population going twice a week to the cinema. World events made little impact, for there was no television as yet to bring instant images of calamity, and the wireless and the daily press were not like today's powerful media. To most people, the dark clouds of war on the horizon were hardly visible.

The sort of elementary education I had received would eventually disappear. Whatever may be said of its limitations, which I was too immature to recognise, it had been the sole organised educational experience in the lives of three-quarters of the nation's children. A succession of elementary school teachers, who themselves were the products of this type of schooling, exerted an enduring influence. The individual pupil had to learn to write legibly; spell correctly; add, subtract, multiply, divide; read with fluency both silently and aloud; and above all pass the Grammar School entrance examination. If all these aims were met, the school had done its job; and if you had the right support at home, you stood an even better chance.

One Saturday morning during the Summer of 1937, when I came home after playing in the next street, Mother announced, 'Mr Kenyon has been to see me.' I held my breath, expecting to be in trouble. 'You've passed your scholarship to go to the Grammar School.' So had several of my schoolfriends, as I was soon to learn. 'That's good,' I said, and I rushed off again to play football.

3

The Realms of Gold

... the great ocean of truth lay all undiscovered
before me.

Isaac Newton, 1720

The monopoly for sale of school uniforms was shared by
two drapers, who co-existed amicably in the same street
near the town centre. By cautious purchasing from each,
supplemented by one or two bargains from the Co-op in the
less fashionable part of the town, I was kitted out for the
Queen Elizabeth's Grammar School, Gainsborough.

Now, for the first time in my life, at the age of 11, I was
the owner of a proper pair of football boots. Once I had
tried them out, I soon learned to move with agility despite
their enormous weight. The steel toecaps were heavy
enough to break an opponent's leg. The thick uppers had to
be worked into resilience through liberal applications of
dubbin. This was a chore to which I took readily.

At last I became a pupil at Father's old school. Thirty
years before me, his daily journey had involved a ten-mile
train ride from his native village of Misterton, followed by a
two-mile walk from the railway station to the school. In
contrast, I was less than ten minutes' walk away. Father had
been a fee-paying pupil for only a few years as family funds
were limited, whereas I as a scholarship boy had better
prospects. Such a thought at that stage did not enter my
head.

My contemporaries and I in Form 1A, a mixed bag from town and country, quickly assessed the strengths and weaknesses of our new teachers. The worst behaviour we could get away with was in Geography, which was taught in an ordinary classroom as the school had no specialist accommodation apart from two modest laboratories. We were usually allocated to the classroom of our rivals, Form 1B, and as we sat confined in their desks each of us would quietly produce a geometrical compass and begin to pick surreptitiously at the padlock securing the desk-lid, as soon as the teacher turned his back to write on the blackboard. Like apprentice felons, we mastered the quick flick that released the lock, and within seconds it was possible to disarrange the entire contents of the desk, to close the lid, and to replace the padlock in seconds before the master turned back to face the class. Being slightly deaf, so we thought, he failed to hear the clicking and scuffling.

Later during that first year our Geography master was still busy writing on the blackboard but eyeing us more closely than before. We never knew if our behaviour had been rumbled, and we even began to fear that something was being deliberately held in store for us. Our lock-picking ceased. By that stage, some of us began to take an interest in what was being written on the board. Through careful copying, we became adept at taking notes, as if won over by the careful arrangement of tabulated matter and the use of coloured chalk to highlight key words and phrases. At last we were starting to learn.

I enjoyed most subjects in the timetable during that first year, but the highlight was Wednesday afternoon games when we played soccer on a proper pitch, and indeed on a three-quarter sized pitch better suited to the slighter frames and thin legs of pre-adolescent boys. My competence in dribbling with the ball was usually countered by the sheer number of unco-ordinated players who could not cope with the ball when they received it. Performances in general did not match intentions, yet the rough-and-tumble of physical activity was enjoyed by all. The only other sporting activities during the year were cross-country running, which I found less pleasurable, and cricket. Despite my admiration for Don Bradman and his like, I wielded a bat with only limited success, still bowled badly, and hated fielding in the slips. The scars on my shinbone are a testimony to my incompetence as a fielder, but I never minded being black and blue after a soccer match, whether I had played well or badly. There was little real coaching for any sporting activity, only an assumption that you should enjoy it and have natural skill.

One academic subject that I quite enjoyed in my first year was Latin. Our textbook was based, in its early chapters, on a Roman home, with Pater, Mater, Filius and Servus – otherwise Father, Mother, Son and Servant or Slave. There was some mention, too, of Filia – daughter. Pater and Mater saw to it that Filius, their worthy son, applied himself to his studies: if he did not, then the Slave was empowered to hit him with a rod. Boys like myself, accustomed to punishment at school, did not find this too remarkable, but this strict approach to learning was to become a reality in the second year when our Latin teacher was none other than our Headmaster.

It was a sign of the fear we had for the Headmaster that we seldom made jokes about his name, which suggested that he had an extensive posterior. His Latin lessons were delivered in a small classroom immediately opposite his study, to which transgressors could be quickly transferred for a good caning. One of my few surviving school notebooks illustrates this learning system with a drawing of THE HEAVY HAND, as a general warning, supplemented by a picture of the cane descending with a WHARK. These hieroglyphics are placed against a passage of notes describing the use of the FUTURE INFINITIVE and THE ACCUSATIVE form of the personal pronoun, BOTH OF WHICH MUST BE USED to indicate one's hope, or promise, or threat to do something in future time e.g. I hope to come = *spero ME venturUM esse* . . . Failure to observe this rule in translation meant instant punishment. Anyone who knows no Latin, nor anything about grammar – some of us were in that category as fear stifled our recall of such knowledge – will understand our bewilderment and imagine the pain. Never mind the future: it was here and now that we were suffering.

Somehow we learned to cope with this particular style of learning, having quickly realised that it was simply a matter of obeying the rules and requirements without hesitation or fear. Some respite was still possible in other subjects, where masters whose rule was less repressive failed to eradicate such offences as 'not keeping quiet when told', or 'not submitting homework on time'. The first offence merited 'lines', writing out 'I must not...' 100 or 200 times; the second offence led to 'detention', being kept in school for an extra period at the end of the afternoon. This was, as it turned out, a good opportunity to get one's homework done.

The frequency of offences punished by 'lines' stimulated one of my first entrepreneurial activities. I discovered, after having had my own share of 'lines' for minor offences in the classroom, such as talking when not required, or doing the wrong piece of work, that with a number of pens clamped together in parallel and a little crafty manipulation several lines could be written simultaneously. I experimented with arrangements of three or four pens, and offered my services at sixpence per hundred lines. After some modest receipts, business began to dwindle as conformity to the school system became stronger and lessons were being taken more seriously.

Leisure time away from school provided an escape from the demands of the school syllabus, particularly into the world of Dick Tracy, Superman, and other transatlantic heroes. It was thanks to our next door neighbour, whose relative in Canada sent the 'funnies' at regular intervals, that I was introduced into the colourful world of adventure and fantasy presented through this weekly newspaper cartoon supplement. It was almost a catastrophe if the next edition failed to arrive. Sometimes two or even three issues came together, and it needed much self-restraint not to look first at the latest episode to find the outcome of some cliff-hanging situation. Unfortunately within a year or two, because of the advent of war, the supply would dry up.

Much as I enjoyed spending time reading the 'funnies', I was always looking for a chance to be physically active. At one period, several of my friends and I took to roaming the neighbourhood at dusk, dressed as phantoms of the night in home-made face masks and torn-up old curtains fashioned into cloaks. We would rush suddenly out of concealment to confront any pedestrians in the vicinity, expecting to terrify anyone in our path. The reality was that most of those accosted, apart from smaller children than ourselves, were more annoyed than frightened. We were always instantly recognised by all the grown-ups, who to their credit were tolerant enough not to complain to our parents.

Pranks by young schoolboys were, at the time, of little consequence compared to what was beginning to happen in the wider world. There were constant references on the wireless and in the newspapers to alarming events in Europe. Adolf Hitler's forces had marched into Czechoslovakia. There was something called 'appeasement' that had not succeeded. Then there was trouble in Poland, the loss of the Polish corridor, whatever that was, and all the adults were talking about an agreement signed in Munich that had failed. Unless Adolf Hitler changed his policies of grabbing more territory, there was going to be a war, but this was not really understood by schoolboys at that stage.

To most of us these were only external stirrings around the closed world of school, where the traditional pursuit of learning governed all. At the end of the Summer term, when the whole school assembled to hear the Headmaster read out the class orders based on the term's work and the examinations, I waited patiently for the results of Form 2A. By the time seventh had been reached, I was still not mentioned. At last it came out: third, Hastings K. N. We had already been told that the top three would be jumped next term into Form 4.

My thirteenth birthday, my jump into the fourth year, and the outbreak of World War Two were about to co-incide. I clearly remember the solemn tones of Neville Chamberlain announcing on the wireless that Adolf Hitler had not kept his promise to do what he should, or should not, have done, and 'consequently this country is at war with Germany.' We were soon to hear the sound of air-raid warning sirens, as a practice, but we could not imagine what the real thing would be like. A more frightening prospect was that poison gas bombs would be dropped. People began to envisage simultaneous strikes throughout the country. We did not know that such capability was beyond the power of Nazi Germany at that time. Nevertheless, in true British style, men, women and children trooped off to the Town Hall to be issued with gas masks. Instructions were given on how to seal up domestic windows and air bricks to prevent the entry of poison gas. This provided yet another opportunity for my emerging entrepreneurial skill. Following the approved recipe, I made buckets of papier-mâché and proceeded to slosh the mixture onto the outside of all the air bricks of our house at ground level and over the inside gaps of the various sash windows. I then performed this service for some of our neighbours and received a few sixpences in return. Later on, strips of gummed brown paper were stuck on all window panes to prevent the glass shattering from bomb blasts. This time the task was left to others, but its effectiveness was never to be tested in our part of the town.

Other measures were to follow, such as the erection of black curtains to obscure all light from outside view during the hours of darkness, and the masking of lights on vehicles, including bicycles, so that only thin strips of illumination could be seen. This was the time of the so-called 'phoney war', when proper confrontations between opposing forces had not yet begun, and life had some semblance of normality.

My arrival in Form 4A introduced me to a different and difficult world. Unfortunately, despite the system of jumping the top boys from year 2 to year 4, no special intermediate or bridging tuition was provided. We were plunged straight into the usual curriculum and left to make up the distance. We also now had to cope with masters of different style, who offered no happy mean between a constant spate of dictated notes and none at all. One master intrigued me because of the irregular specks of white froth at the side of his mouth. Possibly he was sucking indigestion tablets. His knowledge of history was immense, but it seldom came across at a level I could take in, despite the copious notes. Throughout the time when the British Expeditionary Force was fighting impossible odds prior to the evacuation from Dunkirk in 1940, he stuck resolutely to the events of the Seven Years War, 1756 to 1763, and then, curiously, to the legacy of Confucius, who hitherto was known to us only through some rather feeble schoolboy jokes. There were no diversions to comment on the real war that was going on. Many years later, when I was to teach History briefly for GCE, I found out the hard way how demanding it is to teach historical events and to stimulate the ability of immature minds. The hardest task of all is to evaluate contemporary events. To his credit, our History master scored at sixth-form level, where he had many notable successes. One of his star pupils later became a university professor.

A greater problem presented itself outside the classroom. A group of bullies had emerged. I and one or two other boys were amongst its victims, whenever we could be forced into the more secluded part of the school grounds. This was the first time I had ever been pushed around at school and deliberately roughed up. There were no masters around when the action started, nor was it the done thing to seek their help. The threat of more punches tomorrow added to the pain of today. Mother began to comment on the amount of mud on my clothes. When I was eventually forced to explain, there was no question of either parent writing a note of complaint or daring to confront the Headmaster.

In the end the problem solved itself. The bullies found other outlets for their energies, or perhaps outgrew the urge, or were distracted by a radical change in the school programme, with the introduction of a half-time school day to enable our facilities to be used by a large contingent of boys from another secondary grammar school in Leeds. This was a not uncommon arrangement in the early stages of the war. We went to school in the morning; they went in the afternoon. It must have taken an extraordinary adjustment of the timetable, and no doubt had a retarding effect in some parts of the curriculum. The bonus was more time in the other half of the day to play games, and to complete one's homework comfortably.

There was great excitement in September 1940, when we moved into brand-new buildings on the outskirts of the town. At last we had our own playing fields, gymnasium, specialist classrooms and laboratories, and an impressive assembly hall with full stage facilities for drama. A number of new masters and a new Headmaster awaited us. The dual school usage continued for a few months more, until eventually the scheme was abandoned and the other contingent returned to Leeds. Now everything was in our favour, despite the fact that there was a war in progress. The 'Battle of Britain', which was then being fought in the skies over southern England, had the reality of a distant test match, with the scores in our favour being greeted with acclaim on the wireless and in the daily press. It was to take a few more years of war before schoolboys really understood Winston Churchill's tribute to the fighter pilots of the Royal Air Force: 'Never in the field of human conflict was so much owed by so many to so few.' In a few years' time many of us would depart for war service, but in the meantime there were academic realms to be explored.

Our new Headmaster, F. W. Lockwood, was a revelation, totally unlike his predecessor. Apart from his provocative but light-hearted dismissal of the sciences, he seemed to personify the educated gentleman. He was a Cambridge graduate, a status in those days regarded with great awe. It was this time our good fortune to be taught Latin by the Headmaster, and to be introduced for the purpose of the School Certificate Examination to selected passasges from the *Tristia* of Ovid and the *Gallic War* of Julius Caesar. At last Latin was about real people and events. We also began to glimpse that the Latin language itself has an economy and a logical structure that cannot always be matched in English, though at that stage we were still wrestling with the subtleties of grammar but without the heavy hand.

I was now old enough to note with interest that Ovid had written a discourse on *The Art of Love*, which of course was not a prescribed text. Equally interesting to our adolescent minds was the news that Ovid had been banished for improper conduct, about which scholars had been left to speculate, with one of the theories being that he had unwittingly seen the Emperor's daughter, Livia, in her bath. We had no literature to tell us more. As for the *Tristia*, which were his writings in exile, they only hinted at his dark deeds. The rendering of the Latin text was hard work, and I was astonished by the felicitous translations that issued effortlessly from the Headmaster whenever we were stuck. Our introduction to the writings of Julius Caesar was equally stimulating, relating to our more aggressive instincts. I identified wholeheartedly with the Ancient Britons who had stained themselves with woad, an indigo dye made from plants, in order that they might be '*horrificiores*' – the more horrible in appearance. Somehow, too, the account of the British under their Leader Cassivellaunus fighting the foreign enemy by means of guerrilla warfare struck the right note, especially when I was clear about the difference between guerilla and gorilla.

Slowly throughout 1941 the impact of the real war at last began to be felt, even by grammar-school fifth-formers. From January 1941 there had been severe air raids by the Luftwaffe on London and other cities such as Hull, Plymouth, Liverpool and Belfast. The government realised the necessity for a strong air force, and without exactly following the model of the Hitler Youth movement introduced a pre-service organisation called the Air Defence Cadet Corps, open to boys of 14 upwards. Our own school squadron was established under the leadership of the chemistry master and launched quickly into a programme of extra-curricular training. We had regular drill, as well as instruction in navigation, Morse Code and map-reading. The assumption was that all cadets would ultimately gain entry into the Royal Air Force. In due course, at the age of 17½ I was to volunteer for service in the hope of becoming a pilot, navigator, or bomb-aimer.

It was during this period that Gainsborough was unexpectedly the recipient of some high-explosive bombs, dropped by German bombers diverted by RAF fighters. The enemy planes, having been chased into Lincolnshire during a bombing raid on York, dumped their remaining bombs to lighten their airborne weight and to increase speed so as to escape. Gainsborough just happened to be a convenient spot. All the bombs fell near to the centre of the town, demolishing many shops and creating a blast of air that rushed along the narrow streets, blowing out scores of shop windows. The main front wall of the Town Hall had to be shored up to prevent the building's collapse, and it was not restored until several years after the war ended.

This incident, though relatively minor compared to what was happening elsewhere, was enough to make life rather serious. People began to think profoundly – even the fifth-formers. I remember one day asking Father, who had every claim to being a good Christian, if he thought the Germans prayed to God for victory against the British. It would be difficult for God if both sides prayed to win. Father gave a reflective answer, 'God only knows,' for by this time the Germans had invaded Russia, so it looked as if they would need no divine assistance to win the war.

In the meantime school assemblies were calculated to sustain our morale as we lustily sang 'Fight the good fight,' 'Onward Christian soldiers,' or 'Who would true valour see, let him come hither'. During one of the assemblies, marking some special occasion, the National Anthem was played. Everyone dutifully stood up – except for one remarkable fourth-former, who to the consternation of the whole assembly remained seated throughout the majestic strains. The anthem finished. A terrible silence reigned. At last an icy voice from the hall stage said, 'Warburton, why did you not stand up for the King?' 'Sir,' said Warburton, 'Jehovah is my King.'

The point was that Warburton's father, the erstwhile organist at the local Wesleyan chapel, which my family attended, had suddenly shocked, indeed rocked the Methodist community one day by announcing his transfer of loyalty to the Jehovah's Witnesses. The whole family, which included four children, adopted the new creed. I have no knowledge of how the Headmaster dealt with young Warburton's stand, once he had been ordered to leave the assembly and to await the Headmaster's coming. Such incidents were very rare, and provoked much tongue-wagging. I could hardly have guessed that in two years time I myself would be at the centre of another dramatic interlude in the school hall – of which more later.

The art of public speaking, for legitimate purposes, was encouraged in the upper forms through inter-House competitions, another innovation of the new Headmaster. I was selected as a member of our House team, and gave considerable thought to my choice of subject for a five-minute address. From my valued encyclopaedia I condensed an account of how the Chinese had developed fireworks. The interest stemmed from my liking for chemistry and my first experiments with a modest chemistry set. Fortunately I had not carried out the practical blending of salpetre (75 parts), charcoal (15 parts) and sulphur (10 parts), as laid down in the traditional formula for an explosive mixture. My talk conveyed my enthusiasm well enough, and I was given a good mark. More demanding tests of speaking in public would await me in the sixth form.

The academic year ended with the School Certificate examinations. I was relieved that I gained enough credits in English Language and other subjects to 'matriculate'. To my surprise and pleasure, I achieved a distinction in three

35

subjects – Latin, Physics and Chemistry, and I was top of the year in the class lists. The one and only subject in which I failed the School Certificate was History.

The Headmaster's liberal thinking encouraged sixth-formers to mix arts and science subjects for the Higher School Certificate examination. I elected to do Latin, French and English, together with Mathematics, so renouncing the further study of Physics and Chemistry. There had been no question of leaving school and going into employment, nor any overt discussion of career prospects. There was a kind of unstated acceptance of keeping oneself securely at school until the arrival of military service. In the meantime school life was there to be enjoyed, and Mother and Father continued to encourage me to make the most of it. I little knew at this stage that the more rewarding phase of my grammar school education was now ahead of me, yet with the curious paradox that later in life I would question this very system to which I would owe so much.

As a first-year sixth-former, I was not immersed in academic study, and football remained a passion, along with the activities of the Cadet Corps, which had now become the Air Training Corps. My best football achievement was to be Captain of the Second Eleven, involving occasional games against other schools. In those days you did not embrace your teammates when you or they scored. Even more stimulating than my winning goal against De Aston Grammar was the experience of visiting the Royal Air Force bomber station at Hemswell, just a few miles from Gainsborough. On the appointed day, after seeing much of the base, including the operations room and the control tower, we were given a brief flight in an Armstrong Whitworth Whitley bomber, which was used for training. It took some time to get into our parachute harnesses, climb clumsily aboard, and ease ourselves into the various cramped positions throughout the aircraft. I was manoeuvred into the bomb-aimer's compartment, astonished by the noise of the engines already revving up and by the Meccano-like interior of the fuselage. After a thunderous take-off, we circled the aerodrome a few times at about 1500 feet in perfect weather. Later, when I was safely back home, I was quite certain that as soon as I was old enough I would volunteer to join the RAF.

Germany's equivalent, the Luftwaffe, was still busy. Its use of incendiary, as well as high-explosive, bombs led to every neighbourhood setting up fire-watching patrols. These were made up of householders in one's own street who were on duty to take evasive action against any incendiary bombs in the event of an air-raid. Usually people served in pairs, with two- or three-hour shifts throughout the night. Younger fire-watchers like myself were detailed to do the earlier shifts before midnight. Buckets of sand and stirrup pumps were the main counter weapon. Many of us at school had already had the opportunity to practise with these, thanks to the co-operation of the local fire brigade who liaised with the school. We also at school learned some elementary first aid. Fortunately, in our part of the town, we never had to go into action.

The autumn of 1942 saw what Churchill described as 'the end of the beginning', with the battle of El Alamein during the North African campaign. It was at this time, undeterred by thoughts of war, that I was striving to find a happy mean between school work and leisure pursuits. A rapidly growing interest in girls had already led me into the local dance hall at least once a week. Then another entrepreneurial urge led me, as a very unaccomplished violinist with aspirations to become a second Stephane Grappelli, to team up with a strange trio of musicians – drums, piano, bass – who played for the odd local gig. The leader, who played the bass with some skill, had a disability that had prevented his call-up for military service. He did his best to orchestrate our efforts, but these were not the days of stereophonic sound. Our renderings, without technological enhancement, were simple, rhythmic, and quite forgettable, including a great number of popular hits of the day. 'Praise the Lord, and Pass the Ammunition', 'You are My Sunshine', and 'The Singing Hills' are but three titles I recall. I was paid several shillings for a night's work in the Co-op Hall. By this point in the war all competent musicians, indeed all men with competence, had been called up, so there was not much competition. Eventually, one of these gigs took place in the Grammar School on a Saturday night. Something prompted the Headmaster to look in during the evening. His face was a study when he spotted me sawing away, but there were no words of discouragement when we next met.

Late in December of that year I was suddenly taken ill as a result of a pelvic abscess. The experience of hospital was somewhat traumatic, mainly because I was near to an elderly patient who was dying. He was discreetly removed to a side ward during his final hours, but it was impossible not to hear his death rattle. Such events, however, did not deter the general celebration of Christmas. I gained a new respect for nurses and developed a fancy for one or two of the more flirtatious probationers. I left hospital also with a greater understanding of mortality. A few months later I returned to have the appendicectomy which it had not been possible to perform on the earlier occasion. This time there were no deaths, and I was impressed by the regal manner and efficient control of Matron Kelly, for whom all patients, if capable, sat to attention in bed during her daily rounds. The medical staff, doctors and nurses alike, responded obediently to her call.

With these interludes behind me, I continued to move through the ups and downs of adolescence. As I sought to discover there was more to life than school, Mother and Father were tolerant and helpful. They usually encouraged me to bring friends home, particularly girls, who were never made to feel they were under scrutiny, which of course they were. In matters of smoking and drinking, habits which could hardly be avoided in the close encounters of wartime socialisation, they encouraged me to smoke occasionally at home instead of frequently in public and to accustom myself to alcohol with discretion. Father had been very upset when he first learned of my visit to a pub, but he accepted that I was getting to be old enough to make my own decisions. In fact it was at this period that I first began to appreciate my parents in a much deeper way. They were always willing to be drawn into discussion on any issue that vexed me, whether it was to challenge the existing codes of morality or politics, or to wonder whether we would all emerge unscathed from the war.

At the end of the academic year, my Higher School Certificate results were reasonable without being brilliant. I had the equivalent in today's gradings of B in English and C in the rest. These results were enough to earn me a Lindsey Senior Scholarship. With this financial aid, I was then ready for my final and formative year at school as a third-year sixth-former.

As an added bonus I had been appointed Head Prefect. In my favour for this office was my previous role as Head of Hickman House, one of the four school houses. To the annoyance of the others, Hickman had forged ahead in all the inter-House competitions, and by the following summer had won 11 of the 17 trophies, including all the cups for cricket and soccer. Being Head Prefect provided the close contact with staff and pupils that encouraged self-confidence, as well as diplomacy and initiative. Even one's fellow prefects, the symbols of authority, could be disruptive, and there were several occasions when I had to negotiate with the Headmaster to reduce his displeasure, which was usually short-lived. He was always a model figure, dispensing justice with humanity, taking a keen interest in all his pupils throughout the school, and exuding a lively sense of humour.

Once again Latin literature, as taught by the Headmaster, was full of the stuff of humanity. The *Satires* of Juvenal seemed timeless in application, with his descriptions of Roman society and culture in decline, so that the people craved for only two things, '*panem et circenses*' – or bread and the circuses, equivalent to the dole and the dogs. I was particularly taken also with his reflection that poverty has no unhappier feature than that it makes people the object of ridicule. Likewise in the *Agricola* of the historian Tacitus I was moved by the stark truth of '*solitudinem faciunt et pacem appellant'* – they make a wilderness and they call it peace, for this was the image of Occupied Europe in our own time of war.

Despite my academic occupation, I was still aware of the prospect of military service. I decided to volunteer for the RAF. There were no parental objections. The process finally involved several written tests and a medical. I passed the first, and failed the second because of partial colour-blindness. This was something that had hitherto escaped detection, common though it is. In due course, I tried again, this time for the Navy, and was similarly turned down. Finally, I discovered it was possible to get into the Army as a potential officer, beginning with a special University Short Course. This time I was accepted, and destined to be at Manchester University in the autumn of 1944. As an essential preliminary, I was officially attested at Lincoln Army recruiting office on 24 April, when I swore 'by Almighty God to be faithful and bear true allegiance to His Majesty King George the Sixth, His Heirs, and Successors, and in duty bound, honestly and faithfully defend His Majesty, His Heirs and Successors, in Person, Crown, and Dignity against all enemies, and observe and obey all orders of His Majesty, His Heirs, and Successors, and of the Generals and Officers set over me.' I had passed the Army medical as A1. There was no colour vision test.

It was during this same school year that my French studies also took on a deeper meaning, thanks to a young and enthusiastic Welsh teacher who had studied in Paris and spoke French with a very impressive accent. Encouraged by him, I improved my own pronunciation and grasp of the language. At the same time, I began to listen to the cryptic messages broadcast by the BBC to members of the Resistance and other patriots in Occupied France. Many of these messages in 1943 related to the setting up of escape routes for British and Allied airmen who had been shot down during bombing raids on enemy territory. I could only imagine at that time, without the hindsight of postwar memoirs, films and television programmes, just what acts of heroism were being demanded. These messages became more frequent and cryptic in the months leading up to D-Day in June 1944, by which time Resistance forces were playing a crucial role in disrupting German Army installations and communications. It was not secret knowledge even then that British agents were being parachuted into France, but one could only guess at the everyday realities.

My other major academic study, English Literature, was producing a similar heightening of sensibilities. We had the good fortune to be taught by the Headmaster's father, Mr R.E. Lockwood, who had previously retired after a teaching career in the West Country and had come to Lincolnshire to be near his son. For the first time in my whole school career, I was introduced to a really disciplined study of literary texts, whether in Chaucer, Shakespeare, Jane Austen or Thomas Hardy. I began to sense what Keats was describing when he wrote of 'realms of gold' around which he travelled. I began to improve my analyses of characters and plot, and to explore language itself. I was chastened to learn that one's best efforts can still be refined, or even discarded as Doctor Samuel Johnson advised: 'Read over your compositions, and whenever you meet with a passage which you think is particularly fine, strike it out.' On the whole, of course, I was not disposed to too many deletions because it was sometimes hard enough to produce a piece of work, let alone revise it, yet I was never wholly satisfied with what I achieved. Nevertheless, I was rather pleased one day when one of my essays received the comment, 'This is the best work you have done,' which might not have meant too much, except for the addendum 'and it is alpha standard.'

Despite the academic syllabus, there were other challenges. The climax of extra-curricular achievement that year was a production of John Drinkwater's play, *Abraham Lincoln*. The central role was brilliantly performed by a fellow pupil, Arthur Harrison, who physically bore a striking resemblance to the President. It was a remarkable achievement for this cast of adolescent boys to convey with conviction the conflict underlying the American Civil War, the task of reconciling the opposing parties, and the unexpected horror at the end of the play of Lincoln's assassination. My own role was that of Chronicler, stepping forward before, between, and at the end of the action to comment, like a Greek Chorus, on the cosmic significance of these events. I remember the excitement of moving across the darkened stage, waiting for absolute silence, dimly discerning the rows of expectant parents, and then hoping I could deliver the lines just as I had been coached, with the right pitch, pace, pauses, emphasis and expression. This was especially vital at the end of the play where Lincoln's life is over:

Now [BIG PAUSE]
he belongs to the ages [SIMPLY AND
    TRIUMPHANTLY].

Then the text continues:

> Events go by. And upon circumstance
> Disaster strikes with the blind sweep of chance
> And this mimic action was a theme,
> Kinsmen, as life is, clouded as a dream . . .
> But as we spoke, presiding everywhere
> Upon events was one man's character,
> And that endures; it is the token sent
> Always to man for man's own government.

Stirring stuff indeed in time of war, confirming the conviction that government of the people, by the people, for the people, shall not perish from this earth.

There was an anticlimax to this final year which still bothers me when I recall it. The night before the last day of the summer term, we held a private party in school for sixth-form leavers. The Head had generously agreed to this. The next morning, when the whole school was assembled in the Hall and the Head was only just into the proceedings, he suddenly stopped, looking aghast. Following his gaze, we all looked through the tall side windows and read the huge message daubed in whitewash on the roof of the nearby classroom block: ABANDON HOPE, ALL YOU WHO ENTER HERE. Only a very erudite scholar would know that this quotation from Dante should have read: Abandon *all* hope, you who enter here. I doubt if such a thought occurred to our learned Headmaster at that moment. He turned quietly to the Head Prefect.

'Hastings, do you know anything about this?'

'Yes, sir.'

After a prolonged pause the Headmaster withdrew, motioning Hastings and prefects to follow. The assembly waited in absolute silence.

A few minutes later, we all returned. No further unusual word was said in public. The assembly was dismissed. Many words of recrimination were then spoken in privacy, and the offensive message was promptly expunged.

To this day I cannot exactly recall the events of the night before. Had we consumed too many bottles of clandestine beer? Were we overcome with sudden pessimism at the thought of serving God, King and country? Or were we just foolish adolescents, not yet mature enough in our ways? One thing was clear – we all shared the blame, and the shame.

Despite this, 'events go by', as John Drinkwater had said. My school career was now at an end. A few weeks later, my Higher School Certificate results turned out slightly better than the year before, two Bs this time, with two Cs. I was allocated school prizes for the highest marks in English Essay and Spoken French.

The Headmaster left the school in the same year to become Head of the William Ellis School, Highgate. After only a few months military service I managed to make a brief visit. He described our reunion in an article published in our former school magazine:

A few weeks ago, Hastings appeared at my door. In spite of his uniform, I almost expected him to say,

43

'There are too many detention boys to go into Room 5: shall I send the rest home?' Lewis and Sayers have also been here this term, and I was delighted to see them.

The rest of the article contained the following insights:

There was a time when the pupils of Queen Elizabeth's Grammar School and I had many subjects in common: I could be fairly sure of an attentive, if not of an interested audience whenever I discussed paper in the playground, noise in the corridor, or even why part of the roof had mysteriously changed colour.

Boys are the same all over the country. Only terriers can match them in the ease in which they fall into trouble and the speed with which they forgive those who have to mete out the consequences ... I should point to the broad honesty of boys as being their most engaging quality ... It is an honesty of feeling more than of facts ... boys more often know what they really feel than do their less savage forefathers: their feelings are less heavily veneered with civilisation. If so, it should be the first task of the educator to preserve their integrity – a task more important than the imparting of knowledge – even a knowledge of Latin.

There are two more facts to record about this man, whose influence would undoubtedly shape my eventual career. The first, as I learned only by chance long after leaving school, is that he had been in the hospital operating theatre to see the surgeon attend to my pelvic abscess. He was, apparently, well-connected with the hospital – probably in view of the fact that he was not a completely fit man himself, though there was never a hint of this at school.

The second fact is that, sadly, this able Headmaster died only a few years after taking up his new post. Being abroad on military service, I had no immediate news of his death.

Then, within another year or two, his worthy father also died.

It was my good fortune to have been taught by two such men. Time has not eroded my remembrance of all they taught me and the values they upheld. I imagine them both respected and happy in the fields of Elysium.

PART 2
BETWIXT AND BETWEEN

The imagination of a boy is healthy; and the mature imagination of a man is healthy; but there is a space of life in between, in which the soul is in a ferment, the character undecided, the way of life uncertain . . .

John Keats

Unless men are given the chance to find out what kind of world they live in, what they have made, are making, and could make of it . . . they will continue to walk in darkness.

Isaiah Berlin

The unbounded self-confidence of the young is often at odds with their anxiety about their own future, about understanding themselves, about their health, about relationships, about coming to terms with the world. Those youngsters today who are fit for higher education often choose to take time off before they settle into student life. They may broaden their experience through any kind of work, paid or unpaid, and move away from home to develop their survival skills and sense of independence. By the time they enter the realms of academe, many of them will already have some definite career in mind, while others will still be deferring the need for choice until they have gained a qualification. On the whole, they are considered to have a practical attitude towards their higher education, but they know that even after graduation some of them will still find no employment. Their future is not necessarily assured.

For those young men and women who left their sixth forms during the years of the Second World War, with even more uncertainty about the future, their experiences of conscription or other forms of public service from the age of 18 formed the next stage of 'education'. Many of them were to see the grimmer realities of life; others died. Those who survived were usually confident of a better world. The idea of education for all and of a state providing welfare from the cradle to the grave gave cause for optimism. One of the most urgent desires on the part of those who had done some form of war service was to get on with their lives.

In the next few chapters I relate my own urge to get on after a formative period of military service, which had later taken me to the Middle East. There I served amid the conflict between Jews and Arabs, prior to the ending of the British Mandate in 1948. It was not until long after demobilisation that I began to think less emotively about that conflict, ready to seek a better understanding of the world at large. As I tried to understand the post-war world, I wanted to know why people in general were so happily ignorant, drifting along, as George Orwell said, 'like Jonah inside the whale, with yards of blubber between themselves and reality'. I started in time to understand the sequence of 'experience, reflection, learning'. I was fortunate to start the process during modest employment, some enforced rest due to prolonged ill-health, and several years of university study in which my own thirst for knowledge developed rapidly, and my ideas for a career took shape. Above all, I was doubly fortunate to enter the state of matrimony and to experience what the poet John Donne described as 'this medicine, love, which cures all sorrow'. I acknowledge the value of that medicine to date.

It was during these years that I also began to develop an awareness of social injustice, despite my own privileged position as a student. By this time I had seen the good, the bad, and the ugly. Through the unexpected opportunity to enjoy a higher education and to move towards a choice of career, at the time when unemployment was minimal, I knew I wanted to help others less fortunate than myself. The comfortable cloistered world of Cambridge, where I lived for four years, eventually seemed unreal. I wanted to get out into what I thought to be the real, ordinary world.

With my studies completed and impatient to get to work, I was poised to become a late entrant to full-time teaching in technical and vocational education – ten years after leaving school, and now one of the last of the ex-servicemen.

4

War and Peace

Soldiers who wish to be a hero
   Are practically zero
But those who wish to be civilians
   Jesus, they run into millions.

Norman Rosten, 1946

A simplistic notion of the soldier had been part of the culture of my childhood. One of the first songs I learned at infant school was a sad tale of deception, 'O soldier, soldier, will you marry me?' The soldier-lover gives his girlfriend a string of excuses for not being ready to marry her, culminating after several verses with the real reason – 'for I have a wife of my own'. For me, this was nothing more than an innocent song, and I was much more stirred by marching around the living room with sister Muriel and playmates to the gramophone rendering of Sousa's marches such as 'Stars and Stripes Forever'. Later, I learned that Father had served as a soldier in the Great War, though he never spoke about it. Just occasionally, there was talk of Uncle Louis, who had died in that same war. All this had little meaning for me until, when I was about seven, I read about life in Sparta, one of the ancient Greek city states. A Spartan boy from an early age was taught the virtues of strength, obedience, and courage. Sometimes the Spartan youth was whipped in public, just to see how much pain he could bear. When he was old enough to be despatched to the battle, he was

51

handed his shield with the words, 'Come back with this shield, or on it.'

In October 1944, I had no such thoughts of unquestioning heroism as I started my military service. During my first night in a barrack room at an Army camp near Liverpool, several items of my newly issued kit were stolen, and after the due process of military law I was made to pay. Fortunately, before any further misfortunes could occur, I was posted to Manchester to begin a course of engineering training at the University. I now found myself with about 50 other confident young men, many of them from public schools. Their ability to move through both military training and academic studies without undue effort was to arouse my admiration.

My selection for the Manchester course had been made earlier in 1944, when I had gone through a War Office Selection Board (WOSB) at Retford in Nottinghamshire. This involved written tests, interviews and outdoor trials. It was a new experience to work in a team, surmounting various physical obstacles that represented electrified fences or mined earthworks – all dummies, of course. Those of us, including myself, who were adjudged to have survived, were accepted for six months' tuition in a range of engineering subjects, backed up with some initial military training. Successful completion of the course was to be a first step towards eventual officer training. It also gave the promise of an automatic return to the University when one's military service ended.

Life in Manchester provided a busy routine. Early in the morning we invaded the Rusholme trams to make the mile journey from our billet in Anson Road to the vicinity of the University, galloping the final few hundred yards to the McDougall Training Centre. Many a kind-hearted Lancashire conductress waived the tram fares, even urging the driver to step on it if we said we were late, which we usually were. By the time we stood on parade during the cool Autumn mornings, we were steaming like racehorses. Later in the day, we were despatched to lecture rooms or workshops, which gave welcome relief after square-bashing and arms drill had numbed our minds and bodies.

One of our lecturers was a distinguished mathematician, the author of a well-known Penguin book. Few of us knew this, and in any case there was a problem, for he was so absorbed in his own specialism that he failed to connect with his audience of high-spirited soldiers. Prior to his entry, the electric lights hanging on their long flexes would be set in motion by the more provocative members of the class. Paper darts would be propelled at intervals across the room. The more thoughtful amongst us paid attention, though this required supreme concentration amid the increasing hulla-boo. I found myself drawn willingly into the manufacture and production of paper darts. Something lodged unconsciously in my mind, to be recalled years later when I was teaching day-release apprentices.

Other tuition took place in the more disciplined atmosphere of workshops or laboratories. As budding engineers, we were to study the strength of materials, especially metals. For the first time in my life I saw a steel rod placed in a machine, known as a tensometer, and forcibly stretched until, after slowly tapering along its axis, it suddenly snapped into two. Like a five-finger exercise on the piano, this was merely an elementary demonstration. It was enough to arouse our interest.

In later lessons, when we arrived at the more complex problems of statics, dynamics and mechanics, I was out of my depth, unlike many of the other soldier-students. I was alarmed, and I knew what it was to feel stupid. This, again, was to be an experience I would later recall when trying to penetrate the barriers of incomprehension that frustrate true learning. In the meantime throughout the rest of the Manchester course, I managed to keep up with everyone in military training, though I did not relish the final academic exams.

In retrospect, this period was a strange hiatus in my military service. I had lost sight of the progress of the war since the D-Day invasion of the continent in the previous

June, and I gave little thought to what might lay ahead. All of us lived for the moment, glad to be fed and watered. We had quickly discovered that there were few, if any, recriminations over assignments not completed or other lapses. Perhaps the academics felt sorry for us, but we were quite content. There was even time for making friends with some of the young ladies in the nearby women's teacher training college. They, unfortunately, were subject to their own institutional regulations, which were designed to discourage male visitors and positively to prohibit them after hours. Any relationships were usually enjoyable but short-lived. At least there were no broken hearts when we finally reached the end of our course. I was relieved to be amongst those who passed.

A somewhat tougher soldier's life lay ahead, starting with six weeks' infantry training back again near Liverpool. I managed to retain all my kit and to further my basic military skills. About my only lapse was on the indoor rifle range. The target was described. I aimed and fired. I obtained a neat cluster of bullet holes in the target area above the painted scenario which represented the enemy's terrain, the rifle sights having been raised so as not to destroy the canvas. The sergeant instructor immediately sought me out, looked with horror at my grouping, and uttered loud oaths, at the same time casting doubts on my parentage. The 'red-roofed farmhouse' at which I had fired was not red, nor was it a farmhouse. My faulty colour-vision had led me astray, but I also had doubts about the competence of whoever had painted the canvas. However, I kept my mouth shut, listened to the abuse, looked suitably contrite, and escaped further retribution.

Subsequently, we all progressed to Number 1 Training Batallion, Royal Engineers, at Clitheroe, Lancashire. Our contingent, on arrival at the railway station, was quickly mustered and marched off to the barracks, preceded by *the* band of the Royal Engineers. Never before had we moved in such perfect step, nor with such vigour and pride. I, the child who had pranced to the tunes of Sousa, was now the real marching soldier. All through the town and along to the barracks at Low Moor, we were cheered on our way by the locals. This was but the deceptive introduction to the rigours of Sapper training.

The base at Low Moor was a former cotton mill, each floor of which had been stripped of machinery and turned into either barrack rooms or training areas. It was a curious experience to live alongside 100 or so other men, to sleep in triple bunks, to move with alacrity five minutes before 6 a.m. reveille in order to monopolise one of the few wash basins, and above all to keep oneself and one's rifle, boots and kit in immaculate order. About 20 years later, I happened to be in Clitheroe and returned to Low Moor. I was shocked to see a derelict building. The parade ground had lost all signs of its whitewashed perimeter. Nature had engulfed it in a panoply of common weeds.

Our training was interrupted for a time by an outbreak of scarlet fever, which at that period prior to the development of antibiotics was rated a serious disease. For a time the casualties were numerous, and unaffected Sappers were confined to barracks. To ensure they did not escape, a special parade was held during which, with military precision, the forehead of each healthy Sapper was marked with a small star of indelible ink. In theory this was to aid detection by the guards on duty at the main gate. We quickly discovered that it was possible to pull one's forage cap slightly forward to conceal the stigma, which in some cases had become an inflamed area after unsuccessful attempts to remove it with every kind of abrasive. The sheer numbers of Sappers gambling on an exit at any one time saved us from close inspection. On returning to barracks before lights out, we were still undetected.

When full training was resumed, we were introduced to the subtleties of mines and booby-traps. Burying your own explosive devices in shallow soil was easy enough, but detecting what 'the enemy' had already buried for you was more of a problem. While the hand-held mine detector might solve the problem, without such an aid you had to probe tentatively with a bayonet or suitable rod. The greater complexities of booby-trapped buildings were explained more in theory than in practice. For those destined to become specialists in bomb-disposal, further training would be needed. Most of us for the time being had to be content with a somewhat elementary introduction to the subject. We had no idea if and when we would encounter the real thing, nor how we would cope.

A different sort of response was demanded when we turned our attentions to the intricacies of the Bailey Bridge. War historians would later recognise that the development of this method of bridging rivers, gorges, or difficult gaps had contributed substantially, if not essentially, to the Allied victory in Europe. Having already come to terms with blocks and tackles, and the movement of weights, we quickly learned to prepare bridging sites with picks, shovels and sundry digging tools, to move and join together innumerable heavy steel panels, and to make a bridge which was jacked up and then pushed out on a set of rollers into the necessary position. The eventual completion was a time of triumph and exhaustion, and a tribute to the patience and skill of the various NCO instructors who guided us through these training exercises. They were just as patient with us when it came to the task of dismantling all our fine work, so that the exercise could be carried out with the next group of trainees.

In the subsequent phase of training, we learned to construct the kind of improvised bridges that could be used during military operations in the Far East, where Bailey Bridges might be unavailable or totally impracticable. It was certainly a different experience to stand almost up to one's neck in river water, trying to fix miscellaneous baulks of timber into continuous sections that would sustain the weight of an Army vehicle. Despite the early summer of 1945, the waters of the Ribble remained rather cool, reducing our capacity to produce the essential knots and lashings. Once again, our instructors were efficient and humane. We responded to their leadership, and we learned quickly.

The sudden arrival of VE (Victory in Europe) Day, after

the initial jubilation, left us all wondering ominously about our prospects of meeting the Japanese. Certain training routines involving the use of the bayonet left us in no doubt, since the stuffed dummies into which we had to thrust our bayonets had been given crudely drawn Oriental faces. The message was officially reinforced when we were told that we had to become NIP-MINDED (Nip being the diminutive of Nipponese = Japanese). This was the first time we had ever been given such slogans to absorb. I continued to thrust my bayonet dutifully into the dummies, of which there seemed to be more and more each time we performed the routine.

The message was even more thoroughly understood when we were introduced to various examples of Japanese booby-traps likely to be encountered in the jungle. Conspicuous amongst these was a concealed pit, at the bottom of which were upturned, sharpened stakes, ready to impale any bodies that crashed through the flimsy but camouflaged cover at ground level. There were other varieties of lethal traps involving low-lying boughs pulled back in tension and released by trip wires at ground level, guaranteed to plunge a sharpened stake through one's body. Mercifully, any confrontation with the Oriental enemy was avoided with the sudden conclusion of the war against Japan in August 1945. No-one in his right mind at that time would have predicted that 30 or 40 years hence many of us, as civilians, would be driving cars made in Japan.

The end of the Second World War did not mean the immediate dismissal of all the armed services. It was to take time for the military requirements of peace to be appraised, and our military service continued undeterred. With Sapper training completed, we began our preliminary officer cadet training at Wrotham in Kent. The most practical, sometimes hilarious, part of this was learning to be a qualified driver. As novice motorcyclists we threaded our way uncertainly through some of the Medway towns, where legend has it that there was one cadet who momentarily out of control rode his machine through the doors of Woolworths, round the store, and out again, causing unparalleled consternation.

Getting to grips with the four-wheeled vehicle also demanded confidence as well as hope. Within not much more than two weeks, we were passed as trained drivers, after continuous tuition that had exhausted the energies of ourselves and our nerve-ridden instructors.

Our assumption that we should now be concentrating on how to acquire the more subtle attributes of officers and gentlemen, when we moved on to a basic course of officer cadet training near Repton, Derbyshire, was quickly dispelled. Large doses of drill on the parade ground were at once administered to eliminate the final traces of sloppiness. Some of us were proud, others dismayed, to be subjected to the orders of one Regimental Sergeant-Major whose voice was never outmatched in volume and firepower. Our massed ranks were manipulated into ceremonial formations that in every way left us breathless. In some ways it was a relief to be sent off for the climax of our programme to a battle school in North Wales, where during a night exercise to the accompaniment of live tracer bullets too close for comfort we were propelled in assault boats across Bala Lake. I can remember being more scared of drowning, under the weight of my equipment, than of being shot. There were no casualties, except for an instructor who was shot in the foot. He was a likeable fellow, so we assumed it was a genuine accident.

It was a relief when we moved on to the Royal Engineers officer cadet training unit at Newark, Nottinghamshire, where we were at last in sight of a commission. The rigours of the parade ground continued as each successive intake worked through the programme, but not without one or two crises on the way. One of the more interesting of these was a clandestine operation by one party of cadets, who during the night purloined the sergeant-major's car, and left it on jacks, without wheels, right in the middle of the parade ground, which was holy territory to the establishment. An atomic cloud of establishment wrath hung over the unit for some time, before it was painfully dispersed with punishments and restrictions that were applied collectively and borne unflinchingly. The much lesser crime of leaving the camp at night without permission went undetected, thanks to a carefully excavated hole under the fence behind bushes at a less frequented point of the camp perimeter. We were Sappers to the last.

In March 1946 the whole of my intake, once commissioned, was sent to Chatham, Kent, where for three months we were given a concentrated course in building construction, with a view to being posted as Garrison Engineers. It was a new experience to be introduced to quantity surveying and the use of the theodolite. With the limited knowledge and skill gained by the end of the course, I imagined that in my first officer posting I would simply say, 'Carry on, Sergeant,' hoping that the sergeant was more qualified than I was. It was perhaps a sign of the confusion affecting military manpower planning at that time that only two of us out of 200 subalterns were posted to duties as Garrison Engineers. I was not one of them. It was equally odd that, having been asked to offer our preferences for posting to Germany, Middle East, or Far East, few of us had our wishes fulfilled. I had asked for Germany, but I was allocated Middle East.

Several weeks later, in June 1946, I arrived at a transit camp by the Suez Canal, where I began to get used to the heat and smell of Egypt while waiting to be despatched to future duties. The eventual news of my posting to Compressed Gas Depot, RE, in Alexandria made me wonder what on earth was ahead. It turned out to be a mini-military equivalent of the British Oxygen Company, and my first commanding officer was in fact a former BOC executive. I was expected to understand the production process instantly, to handle mounds of paperwork arriving through Army channels, and to attend to various general duties. Fortunately, I really was able to say, 'Carry on, Sergeant,' at regular intervals. After a brief induction period, I was posted to Palestine, where the unit had a smaller base at

Beit Nabala near Lydda airport. I arrived with scant knowledge of the long-standing conflict of Arab versus Jew. My understanding was to increase during the next two years.

Neither Arabs nor Jews had been satisfied with the League of Nations' proposals since 1917 to determine their respective claims to living space in Palestine. The Arabs had openly rebelled against the British, until suppressed in 1939, and the Jews had gradually begun their own revolt prior to the end of the Second World War. By 1946 acts of terrorism by the Irgun Zvai Leumi were on the increase, and the most provocative of these was the blowing up of a large part of the King David Hotel in Jerusalem, which was an important centre for British military and government administration. About 90 people – British, Jewish and Arab – were killed. The commander of British Troops in Palestine and Transjordan, Lieutenant-General Sir Evelyn Barker, was so incensed that he issued an order three days later, placing out of bounds all Jewish places of entertainment, cafes, restaurants, shops, and private dwellings. He also ordered that all dealings with any Jews should be as brief as possible. The conclusion to his message was that this would affect the Jews on a way he said they would understand – by striking at their pockets. The outcome was hardly what the General or British troops could have foreseen: there was a great political outcry both in Britain and in the USA and before very long British Troops in Palestine and Transjordan had a new General Officer Commanding, Lieutenant-General Macmillan. Taking in all this was part of my homework as I began to come to terms with life in Beit Nabala.

Beit Nabala had for many years been a large military base, comprising workshops and supply depots. It was a sprawling camp in barren territory, surrounded by a tall perimeter fence several miles long. The nearby Arab village, from which the camp took its name, was one of the main sources of civilian labour, mainly operatives. Jewish civilians were also employed, some as operatives, some as clerical workers, all of whom were conveyed to work by British Army transport from towns and villages further afield. The detachment, to which I was posted as officer-in-charge, employed about 50 Arabs and Jews in two small factories, the first producing oxygen, the second acetylene. Both these products were supplied to the base workshops at Beit Nabala and elsewhere in Palestine. An additional product was oxygen for medical use by both British Army and civilian hospitals. To meet the constant demand for all these gases, the factories were kept on full production day and night.

Few people outside the detachment had any idea of what improvised installations we were operating. Many of the compressors, purifiers, and electric motors were of German or Italian origin, having been salvaged during the North African campaign in the earlier stages of the war. After being reconstituted by skilled Army technicians, they were now being operated by Arab and Jewish hands, under military supervision, with no racial tension and very few stoppages. One of the most bizarre features of this installation was that carbide sludge, a by-product of the acetylene manufacturing process, became a much sought-after commodity. Someone had discovered, in those days prior to the development of emulsion paint, that dried-out carbide sludge made an excellent whitewash. Given the propensity of the British Army for whitewashing buildings, quite apart from the logic of doing this in hot climates, our unit was frequently visited by customers from other distant Army units. Even when the general situation, because of the growth of terrorist activity, became dangerous and the movement of military vehicles was restricted, there were still armed convoys coming at intervals to Beit Nabala – to collect whitewash.

In our own unit, we could fill our time at work without the diversion of whitewashing, but boredom was the great enemy for those off duty. Everyone would long for an interlude when it was officially safe to allow troops into nearby towns and villages. During one such period, I arranged to accompany a party of Sappers on an evening out of camp to visit one or two modest establishments

61

offering refreshment. The main object was to enjoy the temporary escape from Beit Nabala, where the drab environment by day and the howling· of jackals at night as they foraged along the wadis outside the camp combined to make us all feel stir-crazy. We had all agreed to re-assemble for departure within an hour. By the appointed departure time three of our Sappers had failed to turn up, but within minutes they appeared, one of them bleeding from a knife wound, the others looking distraught. It was not clear who the assailants were. Fortunately the knife wound was only superficial and the victim recovered. We were able to confine the recriminations to the unit, without recourse to higher authority.

On another occasion, when we were enjoying a period of more relaxed security, I managed a visit to a kibbutz near Latrun, in the company of one or two fellow officers who had previously made amicable contacts there. Our expectation was that we might learn something of the ideals and intentions of the kibbutz, but a certain language difficulty prevented much rapport with those at work there. One felt that some of the workers saw us as an intruding party searching for clandestine arms. This, sadly, was not a time for promoting Anglo-Jewish entente, since British troops were usually seen as oppressors and often equated with the Gestapo. A hostile message on a wall in one large town said it all: 'BRITISH TOMMY. GO HOME.' Underneath, another hand had written: 'I WISH WE F.....G WELL COULD! British Tommy.'

Early in 1947, while riding to work on a motorcycle within the camp, I collided with a three-ton Army lorry. I remember lying on the road, still conscious, aware of the smell of hot metal, and not quite understanding that the torn trouser legs belonged to me, as various people rushed to give help. The motorcycle and I were skilfully repaired, the former by fitters at the unit, and myself by an Army surgeon at Sarafand Military Hospital. No bones had been broken, only certain fibres badly torn. Five weeks later, after an enforced rest, I was back on duty, by which time the general situation had so deteriorated that Foreign Secretary Ernest Bevin had asked the United Nations to decide the future of Palestine, but this was to do little to reduce acts of terrorism.

In April, after four Irgun terrorists had been hanged in Acre prison, the Irgun achieved yet another coup by blowing a hole in the prison wall and enabling many prisoners to escape. Some months later, after three more terrorists had been sentenced to death and hanged, the Irgun kidnapped two British sergeants and executed them in the same manner. There were fierce governmental reactions in London and several outbursts of anti-semitism in several English cities. In Liverpool, bricks were thrown through the windows of a number of Jewish-owned shops. The Irgun, undeterred, intensified its campaign by distributing leaflets to undermine the morale of the British troops. One of these leaflets, which came into my possession concluded with this message: 'British soldiers. How long will you continue to be blind tools of your rulers? How long will you continue to shed blood for their oil? Demand your repatriation. There in your own country you can live in peace with your families. There in your homeland there is constructive work to be done. Go home – and leave us in peace in our Home . . .' We still wished we f.....g well could.

There was now, more than ever, the likelihood that Army vehicles would be attacked. Whenever I signed the necessary document authorising official journeys, I would wonder if I was signing the death warrant of British soldiers. None of our vehicles ever failed to return, a fact which I attributed to the intelligence service of the Jewish organisations, for there was no point in attacking transport that enabled Jewish employees to earn a living at Beit Nabala. Even so, travelling in small armed convoys demanded full alertness, especially on twisting roads where there was enough cover for ambushers. I never looked forward to my own regular journeys into the heart of Tel Aviv, where I had to draw money through a civilian bank in order to pay our employees. Walking into a bank with a Sten gun slung over your shoulder and an armed escort by your side does not produce amicable relationships with the cashier. Fortune favoured us, because we really were easy targets as we walked back to our vehicles and then sped off back to base.

By the end of 1947, when the United Nations had decided on partition for Palestine, and the British Mandate was scheduled to end within a few months, clashes between Arabs and Jews were becoming more frequent and gruesome, and British troops felt like 'piggies in the middle'. No-one could have foreseen the incident that occurred one day outside our own camp when a bus load of Jewish men, women, and children was subjected to a devastating attack by a force of Arab Legionnaires whose own base was near ours. The origin of the attack was never clearly resolved, but it fell to the Beit Nabala British forces to clear up the mess. I still remember the rows of dead bodies lying in a stark temporary morgue arranged by our medical officer. He was extraordinarily calm, yet busy for a very long time inserting plugs of cotton wool with precision into whatever bullet holes he could find, and bringing a semblance of dignity to this macabre scene.

At last there came the announcement that the British Mandate was due to end in March 1948. During my final few weeks, as preparations for withdrawal intensified, there were opportunities for both Arabs and Jews to exploit the situation as they sought arms and equipment. One junior officer in our mess foolishly sold a revolver, though no-one had the remotest idea how he had acquired a spare one. He was discharged with ignominy after being court-martialled. Local Arab entrepreneurs sent furtive messages through our employees that they were ready to buy any spare equipment, especially electric motors, several of which were not even listed on our official inventory. I decided to ignore such commerce, concentrating on the legitimate purchase through Army sources of enough dried fruit to fill a tin trunk, which was later crated and successfully transported home.

Shortly before I was due to leave Beit Nabala, news reached us that an American oil company wanted to recruit

64

ex-officers of the British Army. The prospect of earning £1000 per month was tempting, for that was about 30 to 40 times a subaltern's salary at that time, but none of my contemporaries was interested, nor was I. Our sole objective was to get back to the UK. In my own case, I was impatient to go home and put the interruption of military service behind me, though I was not clear as to what I wanted to do with the rest of my life. There were even times, towards the end, when I wondered whether we would all escape safely. On the afternoon our troopship sailed from Haifa, there were intermittent sounds of gunfire up in the hills, as Arabs and Jews intensified their skirmishes. At the back of our minds was always the possibility that the harbour might become a target for terrorists, though it was being heavily defended. At last, after several hours of neurosis, we moved slowly out to sea. Eventually the coast of Palestine disappeared from view.

Two weeks later, after being processed through a demobilisation centre near York, I arrived home in Gainsborough, feeling like a Humphrey Bogart stand-in with my pinstriped suit and trilby hat. Both food and clothes were rationed commodities for civilians. The crate of dried fruit was received like manna from heaven, and my wardrobe was to remain very sparse for a few years. After the initial euphoria of coming home, I was simply content to feel safe, and no longer to be sleeping with a loaded revolver under my pillow. I adapted to the cool Spring weather, almost welcoming the biting Lincolnshire easterly wind.

In other respects I could not adapt. I was incapable of thinking clearly about my family, my future, or the world in general. It was as if the enforced acceptance of army routine and discipline had completely dulled my senses. I was not even at peace when asleep, and would sometimes wake up during the night shouting so loudly that I disturbed Mother and Father. At that time I had no idea what would be needed to pacify the buried self that needed to emerge. Yet within weeks I was certain of one thing – that I had to go off and make my life away from home. Mother and Father showed their usual unselfish acceptance when I set off to find employment in London.

Some five or six years later, my parents were surprised to have an unexpected caller. He was young, handsome, smartly dressed and dark-skinned, according to Mother. Recently married to an English girl, he was now living near Birmingham and working in the car industry. His application for British citizenship had been made in 1948 and supported by the Army unit with whom he had served. This, in fact, was Ahmed, a Christian Arab, who had been my regular driver in Beit Nabala. Just prior to my return home, I had signed the necessary papers for his application to become a UK citizen. 'He spoke of you as if you were God,' said Mother. There was nothing I could say to that. Mother also, for once, made no further comment.

5

A Tale of Two Cities

... it was the spring of hope, it was the winter of despair.

Charles Dickens, 1859

Like the country boy seeking fame and fortune, I was soon to leave home, not so much driven by ambition but consumed with a feeling of ignorance as to what had been happening in the world in general. George Orwell had already written that most people are like Jonah inside the whale, drifting along with yards of blubber between themselves and reality. In my case, I had not even heard of George Orwell and I was not even inside the whale, rather stranded on the shore.

I felt as if I had missed something. I had a strange thought like the line of an emerging poem: too late to win the war, too soon to win the peace. I felt too self-conscious to say this to anyone, lest I should be dismissed as arrogant or vain if I tried to explain it. More realistically, I knew I had far to go to catch up with those who had returned to civilian life before me. Now I had to find out what I was capable of, but I hardly knew where to start.

In the midst of this confusion, I began to think about resuming my academic education. I had little information about degree courses and was not sure whether I could apply myself resolutely to three or even more years of study, if that meant being cut off from real life as I feared it would.

I could not see an easy way to test the water, as it were. Suddenly I remembered that as part of the readjustment process for ex-servicemen the Army provided short educational courses. Within days I managed to enrol for a two weeks 'return to study' course at an Army Education Centre near Swindon in Wiltshire, where I shared the comradeship of other newly demobbed soldiers who all seemed to be remarkably cheerful now they were free of the constraints of military life and could test their academic inclinations.

I opted for Politics, which I found of great interest; Economics, which seemed unintelligible; and Creative Writing, which oddly enough only seemed to stifle my natural style. There was something rather tedious about being tied to the classroom for several hours at a time, and the consumption of large quantities of cider in the local taverns at night did little to unleash mental energy the next day. All of us on the course, however, both ex-officers and ex-other ranks, enjoyed the conviviality of a well-run unit. We were happy to conclude that there was still hope for our future mental development.

I returned home with no clearer notion of how to get on with my life, but knew that I would have to earn a living somehow. It was then, on impulse, that I left home to seek employment in London. This was not the Spartan youth going off to war – just a nervously excited young man in search of the unknown, with enough money to last a few weeks, thanks to a generous gratuity resulting from military service. I at least remembered to assure my parents that I would get home to see them whenever I could.

Someone must have told me that Earl's Court would be a good starting point to find digs, which would be the preliminary to finding work. Within seconds of emerging from the Underground in Earl's Court Road I was scanning the various cards in nearby shop windows advertising accommodation – and the services of certain ladies offering lessons in French and other stimulus. Concentrating on the accommodation, I noted a few telephone numbers. My first call to a Mrs Sutherland led me to her boarding house in a nearby side road, and I committed myself on the spot to bed, breakfast and evening meal for just under two pounds a week. Mrs Sutherland, a dour Scot, seized my ration book eagerly, together with a month's payment in advance.

The full impact of food rationing had not really registered with me during my brief sojourn at home, where Mother had regularly supplemented our diet with extras earned on a barter system from local farms. Mother carried out various sewing commissions for the farmer's wife and was usually rewarded with an edible bonus – eggs, ham or butter. Here in Earl's Court, Mrs Sutherland had no such luxuries on the menu and meal times were highly competitive affairs, with several lodgers sitting at a large table on which there were carefully measured portions of margarine and little spare bread. The main course each night was dispensed clinically by our senior lodger, who was automatically given this status because his rank in the services had been higher than anyone else's. The pecking order was accepted without question, but the quickest eaters – and I was amongst them – sometimes qualified for a little extra. Since no-one in England at that time ate lavishly, except for those who used the black market, eating was more a function than a pleasure. Meal times in the boarding house were more notable for discussion of racing form than for the development of any gastronomic sensitivity. For the first time in my life I was lured into backing one or two favourites, and on one occasion won one pound and five shillings. After no further success, I decided to spend any spare money on an occasional meal out. One or two local cafes offered consolation in the form of spam and chips, or sundry delectations on toast that did not invite analysis.

Such was the rule of Mrs Sutherland that she required notice of any absences from the table, or from one's bed. Each expression of intended absence would prompt a quizzical response of 'Aha.' This was my first experience of learning how one simple word could be loaded with such a variety of veiled emotion. There was the quiet non-committal 'aha' without the head-nod that followed your polite statement that you would not be in for the evening meal, and the delayed but slightly more ruminative 'aha' with the head nod – as if to indicate that she really knew what you were up to – after your announcement that you would be away for the weekend. I was to learn that her mind was really on other things, for one weekend when I returned unexpectedly early I was shocked to discover, rather in the manner of Baby Bear whose chair had been sat on, that someone had been sleeping in MY bed. After discovering, from other inmates, that my room had been let for the weekend, I had a curt encounter with Mrs S and arranged to leave. I was thankful that I had not yet paid my second month's rent.

Fortunately I found new accommodation in the next road, where one of the large properties had recently been turned into a private hostel. Bed, breakfast and evening meal were provided for two-and-a-half guineas, which sounded much more genteel than £2–12–6 per week. I took an instant liking to Mr and Mrs Jones, the proprietors, who tried to give value for money and fair shares of food, despite their excessive use of Symington's soup powders, which made all soups taste alike. Mr and Mrs Jones never commented openly on the comings and goings of their guests, and this was a great point in their favour. The main door was locked nightly at 11 p.m., but a late entry was tolerated by arrangement. I was to stay with Mr and Mrs Jones for the rest of my time in London.

Shortly before leaving Mrs Sutherland's, I had at last found a job, having realised that my bank balance was in decline and lacking replenishment. With no clear idea of what sort of work I was seeking, I was guided by an ex-servicemen's organisation into temporary employment as a clerk in the West End. It sounded quite prestigious: British European Airways had bought out British South American Airways, and the stocks of spares and equipment had to be merged. A first step was to correlate the inventories – hence the employment of several scores of new scribes, including myself, to fill in thousands of cards for revised records, at a time when the computer revolution had not yet become a reality on the business scene. On one of the upper floors of a majestic building in St James's Street we toiled away daily, surrounded by mounds of boxes and files, each with his own pile. I use the word 'his' correctly, since men only were employed in that particular section. As soon as you worked your way through your initial pile, carefully transferring details of almost incomprehensible aircraft spare parts from an existing card to a new card, the pile was instantly replenished by a mute but smiling supervisor who seemed to know exactly when you had finished the last pile and were ready for the next one. The production line flowed incessantly. It was a relief to get your wage packet of five pounds or so at the end of the week.

The task was still proceeding by the time I left in the late Summer. It had gradually occurred to me that I was not cut out for a career in commerce, and I began to make enquiries about teaching as a career. I discovered that although teachers had to be trained, there was still such a shortage of them in schools that supply teachers were in demand to fill the gaps. Supply teachers in fact included the unqualified, as well as those who for one reason or another did not want to teach full-time. Those who were unqualified, however, were considered for employment only if they were waiting to undertake training, which meant they had to have been accepted for a future training course. This requirement obliged me to think even more seriously about teaching as a career and to apply to one or two teacher training colleges. By the time I put in my applications, I was too late for entry into a course that year. Fortunately, after a testing interview, I was accepted to take a teacher training course at Goldsmith's College, London, for the following year, enabling me in the interim to get onto the supply teachers' list for the coming autumn term.

The Divisional Education Officer at County Hall warned me, during my interview early in September, that I might find things 'a bit difficult' at the elementary school near to Paddington to which he proposed to send me, subject to the

71

approval of the Head Teacher. When I pressed him, he explained that the last supply teacher had resorted to caning the children on the legs, whereupon they had thrown inkpots at her. After several skirmishes, the teacher had left for good. I was given the further news that her predecessors at the school, both men and women supply teachers, had also not stayed long. I was not told why. With my curiosity aroused, I agreed to visit the school for interview by the Head Teacher. After a somewhat cautious encounter during which I learned little, saw the premises only briefly, and met no children nor any members of staff, as school had finished for the day, it was agreed that I should start the following week. With the unbounded confidence of youth, I felt no anxiety, only an eagerness to see how I could cope with a large class of nearly 40 boys and girls between the ages of seven and eight who would have to rely on me for almost every subject in the timetable, including the games periods which would be held on the roof playground of another nearby school.

It was immediately obvious, as soon as I entered the classroom on my first morning, that the children were not conditioned to come to order on the teacher's arrival. Nothing happened to quell the hubbub as several groups of children shouted noisily or even jostled with one another. They were not so much defiant as merely indifferent to yet another new teacher. I felt more amused than anxious, as if being reminded of my own early misdemeanours in class. Gradually the noise abated as I stood quietly in front of them and they cast one or two curious glances in my direction. At last I was able to start off, and just about managed to control the children and to introduce some lessons that kept them busy. I was desperately improvising as we moved rigorously from one subject to another in accordance with the class timetable which I had been told to follow. I was relieved when the first day ended and alarmed to realise how difficult it was to be a teacher.

A day or two later, Harry, a small rebel with plenty of influence on his classmates, so enraged me by his repeated antics that I picked him up, brought him out in front of the class, and mildly spanked him – not in such a way as to make him a martyr, but merely to show that I wanted Harry to set a different standard of behaviour. The next morning, as I was walking along towards the school, I met a poorly dressed woman pushing along an old pram laden with dirty laundry which she was taking to the local bagwash, the immediate post-war forerunner to the laundrette. She had worked out who I was before I even noticed her, and I was taken aback when she suddenly asked: 'Are you Mister 'astin's?' I said that I was. 'And did you belt my 'arry?' I agreed. Then to my relief, Harry's mother said: 'Well, Mr 'astin's, you keep on beltin' 'im. I don't want 'im to end up in the jug like his ol' man.'

The sequel to this was that I did not keep on belting Harry. Instead I made him a sort of form monitor, and he responded well by handing out books, or helping to collect written work, or tidying the classroom. Harry also had his moment of glory on Friday afternoons when I used to read to the class from Kenneth Grahame's classic, *The Wind in the Willows*. As the children grew to love this tale, they never tired of the more boisterous episodes, particularly the attack on Toad Hall. Harry used to enjoy this encounter so much that he would become convulsed with delight and fall off his seat. This was Harry's special privilege. No-one else performed the same antic; no-one wanted to deny him his pleasure. Usually we would all end up in gales of laughter, such was Harry's immaculate performance.

Most of the children, as I gradually discovered, came from a very underprivileged background. The whole area was one of urban decay, and was vividly described in 'Branch Street, A Sociological Study' by Marie Paneth, a social worker who spent some years in the area during the last war. Prostitution and crime were part of normal life, and not many children necessarily lived with, or even knew, their parents, even moving frequently from one abode to another as the adults in their lives fluctuated in their relationships. On the other hand, some of the children had

73

a more stable situation, with parents who were more ready to question the way school treated their children. I was nonplussed one day when the Head Teacher came into the classroom unexpectedly, accompanied by a mother who claimed that I had slapped her daughter's head. The atmosphere was electric, the children were agog. As soon as I gathered my wits, I persuaded the visitors that we might do better to discuss this matter outside the classroom. It all ended with me having to apologise, no matter what the circumstances had been, and did nothing to endear me to the Head Teacher, as I thought at the time.

It was characteristic of my youthful arrogance that I tended to think of her as a prissy, severe woman with an antiquated outlook. Mrs Stead, and I name her to pay amends, had earned a certain respect from many parents, having stayed in the school for several decades, sustained by her Anglo-Catholic faith and her determination to see that children acquired the basics. Sadly, we had few meaningful conversations, yet she had insights as sensitive as those of Marie Paneth and could have enlarged my own knowledge and insights considerably if only I had shown the right frame of mind. The fact that she was popularly known as Mother Stead was probably more a mark of respect than a sign of derision. No doubt she was the product of an authoritarian upbringing, and she expected her own commands to be obeyed. I felt self-conscious if I realised I was doing anything in the classroom that she might not approve of, such as creating too much laughter or noise, or encouraging the children to work in pairs or small groups.

Fortunately, while I was reluctant and too insensitive to seek advice from Mrs Stead, other colleagues pointed me in the right direction. I learned much from a lady teacher, whom for reasons of discretion I shall call Edna. Edna's status as a teacher was still being determined by the Ministry of Education, as a result of earlier difficulties during her training course and a subsequent enquiry into her alleged political activities. In the few months I knew her, the problem was agonising and unresolved, and despite our more than warm friendship, I never really discovered what it was all about. It was ironical that many years later I was to become employed by the very department that we were both miscalling. Whatever the injustice, if such there was, Edna taught me to prepare lessons and to create a wide range of simple but effective teaching materials for all subjects. We eventually lost touch after my departure from the school, but not before she had arranged for my former pupils to write to me. Their letters made it quite clear that she was battling on in her job.

My decision to leave after only a few months came about quite accidently. During a weekend visit to my parents, I met an old school friend who told me that he was a student in Paris, where he was doing a diploma course for foreign students at the Sorbonne. I was intrigued when he explained that the whole course lasted for several months, but that it was possible to enrol as a beginner for the second part of the course, even if you had not done the previous part. The whole course was a forerunner of the arrangement which some years later was to enable students at British universities to do the first year of their foreign language degree courses at various universities abroad. My Higher Certificates gained at school were sufficient preliminary qualification, and no entry interview was required. I wrote off at once and was accepted to do the second half of the diploma course in French Language, Literature and History. This would take me up to the Mid-summer, and would still leave me two or three months before my teacher training course at Goldsmith's, London. I could see later whether I would need to find a temporary job to make ends meet. With that firmly settled, I then arranged to leave my teaching post at the end of February. It was in this way, purely by chance, that I had found this opportunity to whet my appetite for further learning and at the same time to have my eyes opened to the French way of life.

My sadness at leaving the school was tempered by the expectation of new things to come. I always remembered these children over the years, however, especially when I progressed later into a full teaching career and became even more concerned about the need for a better educational system. My delight at receiving a set of letters from my former pupils, only two or three weeks after I had deserted them, was so great that I have carefully kept them to this day. One of the boys forgot to sign his letter but expressed himself with some style, despite his conventional mistakes:

> ... you read us a story about the cat ho walks by hisself, and also a story about Toad. And they were both good And John Headmeans is getting on oh writ ... and about my friend when we were playing football, one of my other friends kitit the ball and hurt him and the boy kudent walk so my friend went to get a hambles and the boy went in the hambles and went away. and when he came out he said he would never play football and he never.

One of the girls had been to the pictures:

> ... to see the *Glass Mountain* wich wassent verry good all about love, musick, and leaveing a wife ...

which was not quite the right diet for a girl of her age! Several children reported that they had been visited by 'an expector' who had been talking to the Head 'for a long time'. I never knew the significance of this at the time, but other children told me of some interesting innovations – a class 'magerzine', many more pictures on display, and much more singing, which was to lead to a visit to the Central Hall, Westminster. Another boy confirmed this musical development: 'we have a quier in this class and I am not in it and sum othe are not in it ... but Denis and I still go to football.'

Thirty two years later, I had a letter from a colleague who, we discovered through a casual conversation one day, had also taught in that same area of West London at the time Marie Paneth was writing her books towards the end

76

of the last war. He found no difficulty in accepting her account, and told the following story:

> I once had a class of 34 girls aged 14, of whom 27 had been up before the beak for streetwalking! I got into the most fearful trouble with my headmaster because I used to call on children who were absent as, in my innocence, I assumed they were ill and took them grapes! Poor untrained naval officers do some silly things, but my guess is that I did no harm and may have done some good.

My first sight of France had been in 1946, when as a young subaltern I travelled in a troop train from Calais to Toulon. It took 24 hours of slow circuits to move from the many still bomb-damaged areas of northern France, through the central regions, and finally to the humid south, where we were to embark on a troop ship at Toulon, with Port Said as our destination. Only one year had elapsed since the end of the war, and there was still a shortage of coffee, one of the main staples of the French regime, and equally of luxury items such as chocolate and cigarettes. Our train stopped frequently during the night at ill-lit provincial stations, and on each occasion one or two black-marketeers would emerge from the gloom, offering to buy anything we could offer them – whether coffee, cigarettes, chocolate, or even one's wristwatch. Hardened soldiers have soft hearts, so the French profited more than we did. I was quite elated to be able to speak French to a real Frenchman for the first time and to be understood.

Three years later, the French railway system seemed to be working very efficiently as I travelled from Calais to Paris, and then on to Pontoise, some 20 miles north of the capital. It had been by pure chance that I had found out about the possibility of studying in Paris, and it was by a further stroke of luck that I had been invited to live as a paying guest with a French family in this provincial town. I had briefly met one of the family's grown-up sons in

77

England some months earlier, and he had kindly insisted on this arrangement when I let him know of my plans to become a student at the Sorbonne. I was confident that the disadvantage of having to commute daily by train to Paris for my course would be far outweighed by the advantage of living *en famille*. That was certainly to prove true in so many ways.

For some years I had been accustomed to a rather limited diet. In the Army abroad, tinned bully beef had been a staple dish, while cooked meats of dubious origin were occasionally served. Even more recently at home and in London, food rationing had done little to develop my gourmet inclinations. To be introduced to French cuisine was thus a revelation. My hosts were amused that I knew practically nothing about hors d'oeuvres and the rich variety of courses that might follow them. I was similarly ignorant about aperitifs, wines and liqueurs. I was to learn quickly and gratefully, despite my initial lack of discrimination and my meagre appetite. It was observed, with good humour, that I had '*l'appétit d'un moineau*' – the appetite of a sparrow – by their standards, but in the course of time I learned both to eat more and to educate my palate. I was still astonished by the abundance and variety of food provided, particularly on Sundays, when it was usual for family guests and friends to share our table, and lunch would last for several hours. Such occasions enabled me to learn well and truly that '*merci*' can mean '*no* – thank you', but that it is best accompanied by a smile of pleasure and an assurance that you have dined well.

Conversation at evening table was usually lively as the head of the family, Monsieur Marcel, carefully directed his questions at his three sons, his wife, and myself. His wife Claudine orchestrated the responses with charm and sensitivity. André, the eldest son, whom I had met in England, was now pursuing commercial studies in Paris; Jules, a year or two younger, was in his final year at the local *lycée*; and the youngest, Albert, not yet an adolescent, had still to complete his primary education. On good days, conversation was humorous and frequently related to the shortcomings of the English, especially as exaggerated by the Hungarian Georges Mikes in his book *How to be an Alien*, published in France as *Drôles de Gens*. More than once, I had to dispute Mikes's assertion that queueing is the English grand passion. What Mikes had failed to mention was that at least the English stayed in the queue when a bus arrived, and then moved in orderly file, whereas in Paris a group of French people, if they had formed some semblance of a queue, would all simultaneously leap forward the moment the bus arrived. This would be discussed amicably, as would other more salacious allegations – but only if the youngest boy was not yet at table – such as the view that the French have *une vie sexuelle*, whereas the English have only hot-water bottles. It was an education in itself to air the mutual prejudices that have arisen between the 'the Froggies' and '*les rosbifs*'. I was pleased that my hosts always spoke of Meester Churcheel with reverence.

However, on bad days, there were distinct signs of tension during the evening meal. Madame would seem distressed, Monsieur on edge, and the boys would be argumentative about anything and everything. On one or two dramatic occasions, Jules in the midst of a fierce conversation with his father would rise suddenly, utter a few choice swear words – which I would add secretly to my rapidly growing French vocabulary – and leave the room, hurling his napkin into the air as he made his exit. After a long silence, I would be politely drawn into conversation as if nothing had happened, working hard to conceal my curiosity as to the real reasons for all this unrest and attempting calmly to describe the lectures I had attended that day, whether on Surrealist poetry or the economic doctrines of the eighteenth-century Physiocrats. It was inevitable that there would be conflict in a family of three intelligent boys, a sensitive mother, and a conscientious father who had managed to bring his family unscathed through the privations of German occupation and the trauma of war. It was ironical that the conditions of peace now presented a new set of problems as both young and old asserted their rights. These family tensions were something that I, as yet unmarried and without children, could only observe academically, but I found myself torn between respect for the parents and sympathy for the children, and wishing for a calmer environment.

I would soon forget any such problems as I pursued my studies daily in Paris. For the first time since leaving school, I was beginning to feel intellectually excited. The Sorbonne course was opening doors into different areas of learning – literature, politics, economic doctrine, philosophy – and bringing me into contact with students of other nationalities, particularly in the tutorials called '*classes pratiques*', where in small groups we would study a text in depth, or refresh our knowledge of French grammar. In one such group I found myself alongside an American, ex-US Army Air Force, who had bombed Berlin; a German ex-soldier, who had been a prisoner of war in England; a student from Japan, who never once mentioned Hiroshima; and sundry other young men and women from the USA, with beautiful teeth and charming manners. A lively camaraderie developed in this group, leaving one full of hope that nation can live with nation if only this shared experience can be matched in broader matters. Humour transcended all national differences in our common pursuit of learning, our most enjoyable session being at the end of the course, when we were allowed to put on a series of impromptu sketches in which we mimicked our lecturers by reproducing their most common gestures and expressions, especially those of the Professeurs who had proved the most popular.

Amongst these was Professeur Pierre Castex, who was an expert on modern French literature and charmed both sexes with his fluent and flamboyant discourse delivered in the crowded Amphitheatre Richelieu. His analysis of Surrealism in French poetry was swallowed avidly since it illustrated the revolt of youth against the weaknesses of their elders and, later, against systems and governments. Here we all were, united in our desire not only to unravel the mystery of poetic creation but to know whether or not true poetry can be the instrument of a movement or a party, and so enchanted by the Professeur that we would have believed anything he said. The Professeur also introduced us to the delights of Jacques Prévert, an early Surrealist poet, who was still writing evocatively about the often melancholy aspects of life on the streets of Paris, using sparse, simple images of unhappy love or destitution. Such was the appeal of the Professeur's lectures that students were actually queueing to get into the lecture theatre, and at the end of each session he would receive rapturous applause. Professeur Castex himself summed it all up when he explained that Prévert, one of the poets most affected by the philosophy of the Surrealists, had not merely written poems: he had established the climate of absolute liberty in which poetic genius can flourish, enabling us to advance more deeply into an understanding of ourselves. Such a sentiment tugged at the heartstrings of the Professeur's youthful, cosmopolitan audience, all of them in search of truth, beauty, justice, and a myriad of ideals, after the horror of world war.

Yet there were those amongst us, myself included, who were still reflecting on the past, and wondering what it had felt like to be defeated and occupied by the forces of Nazi Germany. Direct questions had to be avoided to spare pain and embarrassment, but cumulative impressions could be formed. Through conversations with friends of my hosts, particularly the younger ones, I learned that many older French people had grown to respect the Germans for bringing administrative efficiency into local affairs, notably in areas where there were no overt acts of resistance and therefore no reprisals. The young had been more likely to want to show open rebellion and had often acted almost too heroically, engaging in what others saw as foolhardy escapades. Yet it was too soon to evaluate what had really happened, too soon to realise that resistance was not uniform, that those who resisted had many different political persuasions and many different motives. Here, only a few years after the war and the occupation, one could still imagine the trauma of the final phase when Paris was being liberated and ordinary men and women of great moral courage were prepared to risk their lives. The bizarre nature of life at that time was brought home to me when, during a visit to some friends of my host family, I was taken to the atelier of an apartment in the Sixteenth Arrondissement to see a clandestine cache of small arms – handguns of German origin, hand grenades, even a sub-machine gun, and some lethal knives. I was too astonished to ask how they had been collected, but I managed to find out why they were being kept there. The answer was: '*Contre les communistes.*'

I could not imagine anyone in England being so neurotic. Then I recalled what I had been learning about the historical divisions in French society, mirrored by the current political instability. There were real fears at all levels of society, and old hatreds persisted. Good French Catholics had already been guided in 1891 and 1931 by Papal Encyclicals denouncing socialist dogma as the negation of Christian belief. The events of war had on the one hand united the French in their desire for freedom but on the other hand had inflamed the very differences that had earlier divided them. In my host family I would hear facetious references to '*les socialistes*'. In my daily travels I would hear heated arguments in defence of de Gaulle who, it was argued, would restore France to its former grandeur. In my lectures and classes I was introduced to the complexities of social and political doctrine since 1789. It was startling to discover that the French historian Alexis de Tocqueville, writing at the end of the nineteenth century, had said of earlier events: 'I had seen society cut into two; those who possessed nothing, united in a common greed; those who possessed something, united in a common terror. There were no bonds, no sympathy between these two great sections.'

Despite these undercurrents in French life, most people had a distinct capacity for enjoyment – '*goûte aux vins, aux amours; tu ne vivras pas toujours*'. It did not take much effort to learn how to '*flâner sur les grands boulevards*' in the words of the popular song, or simply to sit by the edge of one of the bridges over the Seine. One day, when I was doing just that and busy revising from my notebooks for the forthcoming exams, a middle-aged couple stopped and asked in the most hesitant French if I could direct them to the nearest Metro. They looked so pleased when I spoke to them in English, their own language. I had guessed correctly from their quiet manner and their inelegant pronunciation of the foreign tongue. They thought I was French because I was smoking a Gauloise Bleue! At other times, instead of concentrating on academic study, I was in my element strolling through the Jardins de Luxembourg, hand in hand with a special friend, Michelle, who would meet me whenever she could escape from her rather elderly parents. Michelle and I had met through my host family, and we felt an instant mutual attraction, which was now being intensified by the warm Summer air and the general ambience of Paris. Yet I was troubled as I suddenly began to realise that my time in France was coming to an end. I knew I did not want to give up Michelle.

If I was to stay on for a few more weeks, I had to find somewhere to live, as my host family would be going away for a long Summer holiday. I also had little money left and needed to find a job. Suddenly, the end of course exams intervened, with much burning of the midnight oil. By the time they were over, I was sure I had failed. I was now due to pack my bags and I had still not found another billet or any work. Then to my relief, thanks to friends of my French family, I was taken on for a month's temporary employment as a translator and commercial correspondent with a small firm of lens manufacturers in Paris. It was to prove a difficult task. At the same time, after some prolonged enquiries and a final diplomatic conversation with a fearsome *concierge* who could well have been Mrs Sutherland's French cousin, I rented a small attic room near to the Tour Eiffel. In the meantime, it was proving even more difficult for Michelle to meet me because of her problems at home.

83

The first dossier I handled in my temporary post was full of letters from clients in India or the Far East, living mostly in places I had never heard of. I was even more confused than my employer by page after page of rather unintelligible French or incomprehensible English conveying the orders for specific industrial lenses of innumerable shapes and sizes, often mingled with complicated requests for advice from the supplier or complaints about items wrongly delivered or not supplied. I instantly realised that my potential for confounding the situation was enormous, and once again my experience of commerce was not proving joyful. However, my employer sensibly agreed to let me take the work away, with a promise to return it the next day, and I embarked on a daily slog which had me working long after midnight. I was not sufficiently experienced to ask why the firm did not use order forms, although even that might not have improved efficiency. In the end I was making assumptions and guesses which, if wrong, were going to cost the firm dearly.

My private living conditions were not luxurious. My attic room was airless and humid, and the Midsummer climate of Paris was unbearable in any case. I had no services other than a small sink with cold water supply. The nearest lavatory was two floors down, one of the original Turkish-style models comprising a hole in the floor with two footplates on either side. There were probably thousands of students in Paris, most of them in the Latin Quarter, living in similar or even worse conditions. At least I was not sleeping rough like the *clochards*, so I ought not to complain. Yet trying to work during the hours of darkness was difficult because of the very modest electric light, and trying to sleep was a problem because of the noise of traffic below. Worst of all was that I could afford only one modest meal a day, which had to be in the cheapest restaurant I could find. In retrospect, it was as if I was trying to prove that bourgeois comforts were not necessary and that I had to survive alone. I had hardly any contact with anyone other than my temporary employer, and I slowly began to feel depressed and exhausted. By the time my stint of work ended, I was not at all well.

When I met my French family friends again, I had just been to the Sorbonne and found out that I had passed my exams, entitling me to a modest Diploma. My delight was diminished when my friends greeted me with concern and said instantly how ill I looked. They then insisted on taking me to see their family doctor, who having given me a careful but routine examination concluded that I was undergoing *une crise nerveuse*. Being unfamiliar with the medical terminology of the French, I was not sure whether I was supposed to be going out of my mind, or whether I was just nervously exhausted after my period of student life and the strain of the last month. I felt very annoyed with myself for having failed to meet my own expectations, and while I was grateful to my friends for their help I felt I had been an embarrassment. At last I realised that I had better get back to England and restore my energies. I thanked my French friends warmly for their care and concern, and I planned my departure, but not before managing a final meeting with Michelle. It was a difficult encounter, as I could not convey what a really felt and thought. Michelle was in tears, and I was trying to be calm. For once, the language seemed a barrier compounding my own conflict of head and heart. I had to go, and I did not know when or if I would return.

So in less than a year I had lived in two different cities and tasted not quite the best and the worst of times. I had taken a few more steps towards knowing myself, but my end-of-term report was not entirely what I had hoped for. While it seemed that I was able to cope with academic study, I was less competent in organising my material needs. While there were signs that I might make a successful teacher, I would need to be wary of any further commercial employment. Once I could come to terms with my intellectual uncertainties, I might arrive at a more sanguine view of politics and society. Perhaps a few years of higher education would help me to mature. There had been painful signs, too, that I was getting too old for casual relations with the opposite sex, but I was frustrated by not yet having the material security which I thought I needed to support any woman I might love. I had a long way to go before I would be a good prospect, and this was exactly why Michelle's parents had discouraged her friendship with the English student.

Au fond, or at the bottom of it all, Michelle herself could not face the prospect of waiting several years for her suitor to offer the right terms, but she had never said as much to my face. This thought was with me throughout my journey back to England.

When, after my return, I wrote to Michelle, she did not reply.

6

A Lot of Wind in the Cause of Good Health

But now I am cabin'd, cribb'd, confined, bound in
To saucy doubts and fears . . .

William Shakespeare, *Macbeth*, III, iv

Returning to the parental nest for the second time after an independent flight, I was too engrossed in my emotions to show any gratitude. With remarkable tact my parents set about giving me sustenance and care, asking few questions, giving little overt advice, but watching discreetly. It was a relief to eat regularly and well, even though food was still rationed, and I was not asked to contribute to the cost of my upkeep. Yet despite all this, I remained listless and tired, and in the end I grudgingly agreed to see a doctor at the local surgery.

It was the same building I had visited as a child and found so frightening. Now it no longer smelled of ether and strong medicine, and the interior was well-lit. As I waited for my turn, I noticed the worried faces and the muted conversation. It was a relief in due course to come face to face with a young, recently qualified practitioner who was pleasant and confident. It was only when his stethoscope had traversed my chest and back several times that I began to wonder what was bothering him. He began to ask where I had been living, what I had been doing, and how I had been feeling of late, as if to confirm his suspicion that something needed further investigation. As I left the building, having accepted his plan to send me to the town hospital for a chest X-ray, I felt both curious and fearful.

I had never before had an X-ray of any kind, nor had most people. This was 1949, only the early days of the National Health Service. I had no idea how it would be done. One's knowledge of such things at that time was very limited, since the age of television and easy access to all sorts of information had not yet arrived. In any case, I was not expecting to be told very much. Doctors were oracles, renowned for only brief utterances. On the appointed day, to my surprise, there was no doctor in attendance. The X-ray was taken by a taciturn technician, and the procedure was simple and painless. Afterwards I was told by the nurse in charge that I should come back the following week. For the next seven days I was even more anxious, not daring to articulate what I was now beginning to suspect, especially in view of some snatches of conversation amongst other out-patients.

Finally, I was face to face with Mr Donnelly, the visiting specialist. After another perusal of the X-ray, illuminated on a small screen which he invited me to look at, I received the verdict, 'You have tuberculosis in both of your lungs.' There was a rush of blood to my head. For some odd reason I immediately thought of the poet John Keats – he had died of it. So had many other famous people. Even worse, so had many ordinary people, and some of them in the town of Gainsborough. I remembered a voice from the past, a neighbour telling my Father in very hushed tones: 'Yes, you know, the whole family's got it.' Then I was aware again of Mr Donnelly: 'There's a bit of a shadow in the left lung, and a cavity in the right lung.' I was still stunned, not quite taking this in, until I realised Mr Donnelly was explaining the next step, which was to get me into a sanatorium near Lincoln. He would confirm the arrangements for admission in about two weeks' time.

'Consumption', the popular term for tuberculosis, was otherwise referred to as 'TB', and spoken of in rather hushed tones, just as one might talk of someone's death or funeral arrangements. I found myself too embarrassed to have any conversation with near neighbours, and I went out as little as possible. In any case I had no idea whether I was highly infectious, liable to threaten others, and destined to waste away. If I had known then that at that time 50,000 people died annually of the disease, I would have been even more frightened. I kept dwelling on the notion of a CAVITY and a SHADOW, not really understanding their significance. Then suddenly I recalled what I had nearly forgotten – Mr Donnelly's remark that I would need to stay in the sanatorium for several months, but again with no account of what would be done other than to give me a long rest, with as much fresh air as possible. I was too stunned to think what might follow after the few months. Perhaps it was not possible to predict such things. It was a matter of a long wait. The curative drugs that would arrest the disease had not yet arrived. The tubercle's ability to destroy the body was still unchallenged.

Mother and Father, as usual, were outwardly calm and sensible throughout this waiting period, confidently predicting that I would overcome the disease. Without sharing their optimism, I wrote to Goldsmith's College, withdrawing from the teacher training course for which I had been accepted. I did not say why. My thoughts were then concentrated on buying two pairs of thick flannelette pyjamas and checking that I still had one or two warm Army pullovers and some heavyweight socks, all of which I imagined I would need in the exposed environment of the sanatorium. I could not envisage whether it would be like a holiday camp, or a prison, or a barrack room, but as an ex-soldier I was confident I would soon learn the ropes, which for me was not just a matter of knowing all the tricks and dodges but of quickly sussing out the likely forms of treatment. It was rather like, in military terms, making an appreciation of the situation, except that the previous reconnaissance had been severely limited, and the actual plan of campaign was not yet clear.

My first reaction to the new environment was one of

pleasant surprise, once I had been processed and put to bed. I was sharing a small cubicle with Harry, an ex-paratrooper, who nipped out of bed periodically onto the balcony in order to have a quick smoke, giving an engaging grin as he returned. From time to time one or two 'up-patients' – those no longer confined to bed – would drift in for a chat. None of them deliberately meant to tell frightening tales of medical torture, only to warn me about Doctor Thorn, who was rather violent when inserting the needle. It was to be some time before I would learn why, and in what circumstances, the needle would be inserted. The simpler things I learned quickly – how to behave towards the ancillary staff who attended to your bodily needs, how to wait patiently for the weekly visit by the doctor-in-charge, and how generally to keep a low profile. Visitors were allowed three times a week, for about two hours at a time, and the food was very tolerable by the standards of the day, despite the government's continuing policy of rationing. A main priority for patients was to put on weight, which seemed sensible enough as many of us were rather thin, and we were encouraged to drink as much milk as possible. I began to feel more relaxed, and I especially enjoyed the quiet hour which was enforced after lunch, when most patients enjoyed a good sleep. In fact, it was possible to feel completely switched off all the time in this regimented comfort.

The routine of the sanatorium seemed to make no demands on one's energies, with the result that the minutiae of medical supervision assumed ever-increasing importance. You would become watchful of your temperature, since it did not take much effort to sneak a look at the chart pinned to the foot of your bed. BSRs – tests to determine the sedimentation rate of your bood – were kept more secret but talked about gravely. Your sputum pot was another item of interest: whatever you managed to hawk up was taken away regularly for examination. If it showed positive infectious matter, you were in trouble. Only occasionally would you be taken for yet another chest X-ray, though you did not expect to be told the result at once. Then to be weighed weekly would raise the pulses, because you would manage to see the scales and any weight loss would be received with dismay. All these variables enabled the doctor-in-charge to decide the course of your future treatment, but inevitably decisions could not be reached quickly since time was essential to assess the patient's progress. The effect of this was to lessen rather than heighten anxiety, and there was always encouraging talk from other 'up-patients' who would call in to boast of their progress.

Gradually I began to understand the options for treatment, after the introductory period of rest. Nearly every patient visitor to our cubicle had been given the AP procedure – artificial pneumothorax, which was the first option. My companion, Harry, was already getting used to his within a short time of my arrival. The technique was to rest the infected lung through compression – rather like gently squeezing a sponge. The compression was achieved by passing air through a hollow needle into the pleural cavity surrounding the lung. Once the lung had been partly deflated, it would be kept in that state by renewed influxes of air at weekly or fortnightly intervals, resting the infected area and enabling it to heal. At that stage of my stay in the sanatorium, I had talked to several other patients who were coping confidently with this treatment, so when I was at last informed that I too was to follow suit I was less nervous than I had expected to be. The AP was carried out without much discomfort, and no general anaesthetic was needed. I was instructed afterwards to lie on my side and to remain in that position, which I had to do as best I could for several days.

Unfortunately, my AP at the outset did not appear to be quite right. I assumed my discomfort was only to be expected, but an X-ray showed that compression of the lung was being prevented because of a number of adhesions to the chest wall. I sensed that this was bad news and feared that I would be faced with a harsher treatment option. This was colloquially known as Thora, or thoracoplasty, meaning major surgery to remove part of an infected lung, or even a whole lung, a prospect which most patients, including myself, would find unnerving. A few more weeks elapsed, during which no comment was made – it was again a matter of wait and see. Finally, it was decided to give me a phrenic crush and a pneumoperitoneum (PP), which was of much less magnitude than a Thora, and this time the doctor-in-charge did at least explain what was to be done. The method of treatment involved reducing the movement of the diaphragm on one side under the infected lung, making it possible to collapse the lung partially by introducing air under the diaphragm, thus resting the infected area to promote healing. The actual experience proved to be no worse than I expected – the crushing of the nerve was like an electric shock lasting for only a second or two, and the PP produced little discomfort apart from breathlessness. It was a curious experience to have a hollow needle stuck through your stomach muscles to enable the air to be introduced. Doctor Thorn had to take an extra hard lunge to get through. I soon became accustomed to the weekly injections of air and was mightily relieved to be told that the treatment seemed to be working.

Despite these anxieties and the rather secretive attitude of the medical staff towards patients, there was plenty of good humour in the sanatorium, much of it occasioned when patients took the mickey out of one another or out of the nursing orderlies. One such person was Stan, whose real name was Stanislaus, an Eastern European. His command of English was so limited that he was unable to explain how he came to be in England at all, or how he had obtained his job in the sanatorium. This was a time when Britain still ruled the waves and foreigners were regarded as funny fellows, so many patients treated Stan as if he was a Chinese coolie or an Indian bearer, calling him a Berk, or worse. Stan's increasing command of abusive English enabled him to counter insults with 'NO! YOU ARE BIG BERK NOT ME! UP YOURS PIPE! UP YOURS PIPE!' These exchanges usually occurred when Stan was sweeping up litter, whether the Autumn leaves that had blown in through the open verandahs or the bits of paper deliberately dropped by the more perverse patients. A more vital task performed by Stan was the delivery of bedpans, so that in terms of professional advancement he was literally starting at the bottom. He quickly learned to exact revenge on one or two of his adversaries by delaying the delivery of the bedpan. The further insults he took with dignity and not a little delight. I hope Stan prospered.

Apart from these dramatic interludes, there were also more reflective moments, especially on the rare occasions when you might find yourself completely alone, as I did one late afternoon when my companion Harry, who was by now an up-patient, had not yet returned from his permitted walk. This was two or three weeks after my PP, when I was beginning to feel less pregnant with the new inflation. I did not profess at that time to be a religious person, having adopted a deliberate stance of agnosticism some years before, and on joining the Army I had insisted that my identity discs be stamped with AGN (for agnostic) rather than Methodist or C of E. The result had been that I was usually sent to the Army camp kitchen to peel potatoes rather than go on church parade. Occasionally someone in authority would ask sarcastically if I was an absconding air-gunner. Such memories were far from my mind as I lay in bed that afternoon. My mind in fact was completely inactive, and I was staring vacantly beyond the open verandah and onto the horizon, where the sun was slowly setting in a glorious light. I was gradually aware of a strange but comforting calm. My whole being was at one with the universe, as if I had been lifted from my sanatorium bed. Later, I recalled William Wordsworth's lines about 'a sense sublime/ Of something far more deeply interfused,/ Whose dwelling is the light of setting suns,/ And the round ocean and the living air,/ And the blue sky, and in the mind of man.' At that moment I began to feel that there was something I had to get on with, something worthwhile to which I had to contribute, even though I had no way of knowing whether I would succeed. It was as if, metaphorically, I had been given a signal to get up and go.

It was about this time, early in 1950, that I read of the death – from tuberculosis – of the writer, George Orwell. My ignorance of his work indicated the cultural vacuum through which I had passed in recent years. I managed to get hold of copies of *Animal Farm* and *Nineteen Eighty-Four*, and hastened to read them instantly, annotating large chunks of text with a brand new HB pencil. The torture of Winston Smith in *Nineteen Eighty-Four* by O'Brien contained a passage that symbolically exposed the sensitive sanatorium patient: 'You know perfectly well what is the matter with you. You have known it for years, though you have fought against the knowledge. You have never cured yourself of it, because you did not choose to. There was a small effort of the will that you were not ready to make. Even now, I am well aware, you are clinging to your disease under the impression that it is a virtue.' This was like a searchlight on my own worst moments – illustrating the self-pity that afflicts you when you are ill, or the fear that prevented you getting medical advice when you were first unwell, or the apathy that in general dissuades you from any difficult task.

As a further stage towards coming to terms with my own illness, I decided to find out more about the factors that predispose people to TB. Whether this was pathological egocentricity on my part or merely intellectual curiosity, others must judge. Eventually I tracked down one or two published studies, after seeking advice from the NAPT (National Association for the Prevention of Tuberculosis). Once they were in my possession, I kept them well hidden in my bedside locker and covered with plain brown wrappers when I was reading them. I did not think that Dr Thorn would approve. I was relieved to read that TB patients go through many reactions, such as fear or indifference or total unawareness before the diagnosis, and shock, incredulity, shame, or equal indifference afterwards. I was equally relieved to learn that patients can be aggressive, excitable, self-pitying, defiant, over-cheerful or only minimally concerned. However, the more I thought about all this, the more I was convinced that these observations would apply to any serious illness. By this stage, I was beginning to feel confident about making a complete recovery but still had niggling doubts as to whether I was deluding myself on this point. It was not customary for medical specialists in that era to commit themselves to precise forecasts of recovery. My own conclusion was that I should concentrate my mind on the outside world since my physical state was clearly improving.

The general election of February 1950 enabled me to think seriously about political beliefs for the first time in my life and to deplore the divisions emerging in our post-war society. In a notebook which I kept at that time, I recorded my concern that the principal parties fought the election in a negative way, each abusing the other. Thus the Conservatives had claimed that the Labour Party would lead us into a state of slavery (shades of Orwell's *Nineteen Eighty-Four*), and the Labour Party had argued that the Conservatives would only lead us to unemployment and to war. We had yet to reconcile the opposing values of state control and private enterprise, as mirrored in the ideological and economic struggle between the USSR and the USA. I concluded that unless the Labour Party dissociates itself from any Marxist tendencies and unless the Conservative Party avoids exploitation and imperialism, either of the two main parties would gain only a very small majority in future elections. Such were my thoughts after the final results had given the Labour Party a majority of only five seats. With hindsight, it seems I was trying hard to understand the issues, even if I was somewhat emotive. I felt equally strongly about a voting system that requires 43,000 votes for a Conservative or Labour seat, and 292,000 votes for a Liberal seat, though I was not well enough informed to have argued for a better alternative – if such there may be.

On other occasions, whilst confined to bed, I had avidly

read everything I could lay my hands on, particularly the BBC's weekly publication the *Listener*, which surveyed the arts, politics, religion and philosophy at what seemed to me a sensible level for the aspiring student, feeding an intellectual appetite that today would be met through the more serious types of television programme. Thus with the *Listener* I began to reduce my own monumental ignorance thanks to its regular doses of culture and enlightenment. One week I would be reading about the poet Stephen Spender, who reflected by the ruins of the Reichstag on the way in which the German people had been induced to accept a regime that eventually brought them, and others, unprecedented material destruction and physical suffering. Another week I would be reading the argument of a patriotic politician deploring the loss of those older loyalties – God, King and country – and our growing acceptance of a lowering standard of living and a diminishing prestige in the world. (And this, note, was only early in 1950). Later still, the *Listener* was spelling out the daunting problems facing the new government: how to achieve independence of American aid; how to sustain our present level of military commitment, and how to tackle wages and profits. On top of all that there was the need to review foreign policy towards Russia; to scrutinise our educational provision; to reduce social services expenditure; and, finally, to maintain full employment.

Amid all this intellectual obsession, I had almost lost track of my medical situation. It was therefore very pleasant to be given the news, early in March, that I was now allowed to get up for meals, a simple but exciting concession when you have been bedbound for a few months. Before long I received further promotion when I was allowed to dress and actually leave the building, together with other newly promoted men patients. At first the outside air away from the main building seemed like ozone, and it was interesting to see how far you could increase your pace without feeling breathless or having a rumbling tummy because of your PP.

Once that was sorted out, the more interesting part of the exercise was to time your departure so that you converged on the group of women patients also out for their permitted excursions. At first, it was quite a shock to see a group of very healthy-looking females, with ages ranging from 16 to 50-plus, and indeed to be reminded that the sanatorium had its female wing, for the segregation was normally total. They all seemed to be as pleased as we were to encounter the opposite sex and to exchange accounts of their medical progress, including dire tales of Dr Thorn, whose ministrations were endured with resignation. It was encouraging that several of the women patients were due to be discharged within a week or two. Mainly for that reason there was little or no amorous behaviour behind the bushes. This was no time for such commitment.

Just before the end of the month, when I was convinced I was due to get my discharge, Harry and I decided one evening when it was dark to test our infantry skills by creeping silently up to the women's wing to see what was going on. We had surveyed the situation in daylight and found a detour that would bring us up to our target without being sighted. Eventually, when the time came, we arrived breathless and in considerable discomfort after a certain amount of crawling, which was very difficult because of our artificially collapsed lungs. As soon as we raised ourselves gingerly, and somewhat unsteadily, to our feet, and peeped tentatively through a side window, there was a tremendous shriek from the nearest female patient, followed by a sudden hysteria as others in the same ward reacted. We were not exactly frog-marched back to our own quarters, merely escorted by a posse of angry nurses, after which we were confined to our own beds to await retribution. Opinions were divided amongst our male colleagues as to whether our initiative was to be envied or despised. Harry and I felt rather sick about the whole business – mentally and physically, but intermittently like irresponsible adolescents we giggled madly. The worst thing of all was waiting to see what action would be taken. It was not until the following morning that we were told Dr Thorn would be 'dealing with us tomorrow', which meant another night of anguish.

We imagined Dr Thorn would say: 'Are you a couple of sex maniacs? Have you no gratitude for the care and treatment you have received? Do you realise just how much you upset the patients in the women's ward? What exactly were you trying to achieve?' When the time came, Dr Thorn said none of these things but quietly explained that our conduct was inexcusable and he therefore proposed to discharge us immediately. With very red faces, like chastened schoolboys, we mumbled our regrets and managed to say thank you. On the following day, we made a quiet departure in our separate taxis. There was little said, and much concealed emotion, as we made our farewells. Our respective escorting relatives had not, as yet, been told of our misdemeanour. Father was relieved that this was the last time he would be making this journey, one that he had made uncomplainingly by bus so many times, often accompanied by Mother, but he was a little puzzled that I did not look more elated.

It was not until some time after the euphoria of arriving home that I told them what had happened. They were not very pleased, and though at first somewhat alarmed they had enough common sense to realise that I would not have been discharged unless I was fit enough to leave the sanatorium. Of course the PP had to be continued, and so the next week I visited Gainsborough clinic, where Mr Donnelly administered a refill. Afterwards, as I awaited a few stern words, he quickly glossed over my misconduct and updated me on the state of my lungs. He was pleased that everything was now stabilised, and provided I did not do anything silly – meaningful look – there was every prospect that my PP would eventually be discontinued. I could therefore expect to lead a fairly normal life, making sure that I exercised moderation in all things. This seemed a pleasant enough piece of advice as I contemplated the simple pleasures of being back home and having ample leisure time in which to pursue my reading. The discomfort of the PP was minimal, and the only time it proved a problem was in getting out of bed in the morning. The solution was to roll out sideways and then gradually straighten up, as this reduced the gurgling of air and the bouts of belching.

My experience of the last few months had taught me that it is much easier to adapt to the unexpected than I might have imagined. I was lucky that my own treatment had not been drastic – for there were some I had known of who had lost a lung through surgery and then had the other one artficially collapsed. There were also those, as I was to find out some years later, whose infection was of the bovine type affecting the spine, necessitating lying in a plaster cast for months or even years. I was eager to be as mobile as possible, now that I was out of the sanatorium, yet there were always moments of doubt when I went for my periodical refills at the chest clinic and met one or two out-patients who were having problems. On the other hand there were others who were well enough to have resumed their former jobs, even though they were treated with a certain amount of reserve by some of their workmates. In general, consumption at that time was still very much feared not just by those who were overcoming it through treatment but by the public in general. I quickly became accustomed to being greeted with reserve when I met former friends and acquaintances in the street. 'You are quite well then, now, are you?' 'Well, I must say, you certainly don't look ill.' 'I didn't know they'd let you out.' So often, those who are genuinely concerned for you communicate their own fear as they say the wrong thing. You end up crossing the road to avoid them.

I was longing to get on with my life – and to be accepted as a normal human being. Within a week or two of being back at home I suddenly realised that there was now nothing to stop me applying to do a degree course. While I still felt I wanted to teach, I began to look at various university courses in preference to initial teacher training. When Mr Donnelly gave his approval, I then applied to several universities – London, Oxford and Cambridge, opting for degree courses in English Literature. There was no clearance system for applications in those days, and nothing to stop you applying to any number of institutions. I was very disappointed to receive several outright rejections or to have no replies at all, when quite unexpectedly I received a pleasant letter from Fitzwilliam House, Cambridge, inviting me for an interview. My subsequent meeting with Leslie Wayper, the Junior Tutor, then with W. W. Williams, the Assistant Censor, was an occasion when I must have demonstrated enthusiasm rather than erudition. Leslie Wayper, who was actually standing in for Guy Pocock, the Director of Studies for English, was both charming and incisive, and Mr Williams seemed a little austere but was not discouraging. Within a few days, I was informed that a place was available for the forthcoming academic year – to read English. Fortunately, as a result of my military service, I had no difficulty in obtaining the requisite student grant, and I began to concentrate on some extensive preliminary reading.

I was now further along the path to self-discovery and, more importantly, to a greater understanding of humanity and the world in general. Events in my life had given me the opportunity to reflect on my experience. In one of the few really personal passages in my sanatorium notebook, I had written the following: 'When I was in my teens, I was fresh and enthusiastic. I believed that by diligence one could attain one's goal; and because, though brought up neither in luxury nor in deprivation, I always gained that for which I was taught and encouraged to work, I was happy. Perhaps I was too sincere and too idealistic in my beliefs, for the shocks which I suffered subsequently not only challenged them but temporarily reversed them, so that for months I floundered – and still do – seeking the truth, as if this is possible, and gradually revolting inwardly against all unnecessary restraints; seeking to find a sensible way of life, yet thoughtlessly condemning and carelessly overlooking what had influenced me in the past.' There was much more

100

in this vein to show that 'while we need our idealists, we have equal need of our pessimists to challenge them and temper their wild exuberance. Is ultimate wisdom the synthesis of the two qualities involved?' The next four years would give me a special opportunity to reflect on such profound questions – but also to decide on the practicalities of earning a living.

I had no idea then that my treatment would continue for another four years, during which time I would be injected with enough air to inflate a rubber canoe, or even two. Nor had I any way of knowing that in four years' time, by a curious turn of fate, I would be teaching English Literature to patients in a tuberculosis hospital. I was equally unaware that the discovery of three drugs – streptomycin, para-aminosalicylic acid (PAS), and isioniazid would rapidly bring tuberculosis under control, making the artificial pneumothorax treatment obsolete. They were being used only tentatively at the time I was ill. The AP and the PP are now only of historical interest to medical students; but for those who endured them the memories remain.

7

Light Blue

If you trip over anything that resembles a foot of clay, it probably is: stamp on it hard. Doubt is more rewarding than reverence.

Varsity Handbook, 1950–1951

I was impatient to get to Cambridge – and four years later I was to be just as impatient to get back to the real world. In between were the demands of the English Tripos (Part I), the History Tripos (Part II), and a Postgraduate Teacher-training course. All of these stretched my faculties, revealed my limitations, and strengthened my resolve to seek a career in teaching.

As I started my undergraduate life, I found Fitzwilliam House a very pleasant and friendly establishment, and it did not bother me that it had yet to gain full college status. It had been founded originally for students of more modest means than those who entered the ancient colleges, yet it had attracted its fair share of talent, including many from overseas such as a certain Harry Lee, who was later to become Prime Minister of Singapore. However, thoughts of future greatness were not in our heads, as we were directed into officially approved lodgings and began to get to grips with locating the right lecture rooms, the various libraries, and the best pubs, cinemas and tea-rooms. Being 24 years of age and one of the last of the war-servicemen, I felt little rapport with the pink-faced 18-year-olds, of whom there were plenty, acting as boisterously as I had done at their age.

Nevertheless I made it my business to note the range of misdemeanours that ensured retribution by the University Proctors, who in the manner of private policemen patrolled the town at certain hours to ensure that undergraduates were not 'violating the canons of morality and decorum'. I also managed to get a clandestine copy, only out of academic interest of course, of *The Night Climbers of Cambridge*, which described how chamber pots and other indelicate objects are mysteriously spirited into place on the top of certain college buildings. I regretted that I was not quite physically up to trying out the night climbs for myself, but hoped that as an ex-Sapper I could at least give technical advice, if called upon.

After these initial flights of fancy, I soon had to renew my learning role. My Director of Studies in my first year, Guy Pocock, and his wife made me most welcome when I visited their home. Mr Pocock, as I discovered later, had been supervising undergraduates for many years, and earlier in his career had edited various editions of literary texts and poems for school children. What I immediately admired in him was his enthusiastic love of literature – for its own sake. After his tutorials I would race away to various libraries and hunt out books on the Shakespearean stage, or the early English ballads, or whatever the current topic, and look forward to presenting my essay orally at the next session, usually in the company of another student. It was most instructive to experience civilised criticism designed not only to correct inaccuracies but to encourage a more informed appraisal. My greatest problem was that my knowledge was so limited, but at least I came to many new topics with a completely open mind.

My tuition under Guy Pocock came to a sudden end when he retired – deservedly, I hope, and not through the fatigue of teaching ignorant undergraduates such as myself. I now found myself under the supervision of Norman Walters, whose approach to literary criticism was much more incisive and typical of the younger academics. It was a relief to discover that while I was woefully ignorant of so much literature, there were occasional small areas where I was on familiar ground, simply through what I had done at school a long time ago. Fortunately, I relished my first acquaintance with the pre-Chaucerian poets of the fourteenth century, the development of the English novel, and the study of such abstractions as Chivalry and Romanticism. I also enjoyed trying to draw parallels with themes already encountered in French literature and the Classics. The English Tripos gave every encouragement to pursue a myriad of literary routes and its examination papers were designed to test the general and the specific, giving an enormous choice of topics. The only weakness was that you tended to do little reading to fill the huge gaps in your knowledge, as you concentrated on your favourite authors.

In pursuit of further enlightenment I sampled most of the available lectures, particularly enjoying what in retrospect sounds like an in memoriam list – Bennett, Lucas, Redpath, Henn, Burton, Leavis and Sykes-Davies, all eminent scholars but individually different in their ability to capture a student audience. At the time I could not quite understand why Dr Leavis had chosen to dismiss all English novelists except three or four, and why he was so publicly vitriolic towards other leading figures in the English Faculty. It seems fashionable today to decry the good Doctor and to forget the emphasis he placed upon the establishment of sound criteria in writing and in literary criticism. Perhaps I came to him too late to benefit from his particular discipline yet too soon to realise that academic institutions, like all human organisations, are replete with jealousy and antagonism. It seemed to be part of the Cambridge ethos to encourage academic strife, for the resulting creative tensions led to some brilliant evaluation when based on sound scholarship. Unfortunately these hotbeds of conflict propagated many a band of student shysters who exhibited only the passion but not the wisdom of their mentors. On a rare occasion when I somehow managed to get an invitation to one of Dr Leavis's tutorials, I found most of his students were jockeying for position and none could take the lead against the master.

Hugh Sykes-Davies, in contrast to so many lecturers, was a delightful and witty entertainer, whose cleverly contrived examples of English usage illustrated the richness of our language – and its pitfalls. He probably worked out his material when he went fishing at five o'clock in the morning, as he was wont to do, and much of it appeared some years later in his delightful compendium, *Grammar Without Tears*. One of his most memorable sentences was designed to illustrate the difficulty of avoiding the split infinitive and the end preposition: 'This is the oil-lamp my landlady was kind enough to still allow me the use of.' It was refreshing to find a scholar who recognised that language evolves constantly and that correct usage will always be a subject of debate. More than anyone else at Cambridge, it was Sykes-Davies who convinced me that I would one day enjoy having to really teach the niceties of the English language to whatever standard I was up to . . .

The image of the oil-lamp reminds me of my somewhat unusual experiences in lodgings, after which there came a most unexpected solution. From early times, there had been a licenced lodgings system, under which stringent rules and regulations had to be observed, enabling authority to keep a close eye on students' lives. Not the least important part of this system was the regular inspection of premises, to ensure they were fit places for young undergraduates to live in. In my own case I had accepted the adequate bedsitter to which I had been assigned, but after only a few weeks I was directed to move to another lodging. I was not sure whether there had been a sudden official inspection of my current room, with the premises having been found unsatisfactory, for they were admittedly rather decrepit, or whether my tutor had attached undue importance to my tale of a small mouse in the house bathroom that had observed me with undeterred curiosity while I was urinating copiously in the wee small hours. Whatever the facts, or whether my tutor thought I was consuming too much alcohol, I now had to pack my few belongings and prepare to retreat, but not before the landlady's grown-up son, Cyril, confronted me in the hall as I was on the point of leaving. 'You're trying to deprive my Mum of her livelihood!' he shouted. Fortunately, Cyril was about ten inches shorter than myself and about half my weight. I mumbled some form of apologetic denial and left, hoping for better things.

The new lodgings to which I had been directed comprised a sitting room and a separate bedroom in a much more upmarket part of Cambridge. My new landlady was a pleasant, middle-aged widow, who welcomed me without being effusive. I quickly settled there, valued the greater comfort, and was never interrupted when studying. I had hardly been there for more than a week or two when I was once more summoned to see my tutor. With considerable embarrassment he informed me that he had been obliged to make me move – yet again. Apparently he had only just received the news from higher official sources that my new landlady was not a person of sufficient moral calibre to be offering lodgings to undergraduates, for there was undeniable evidence that she had entered into a sexual liaison with the previous undergraduate lodger. I have no idea how the liaison had been corroborated, or by whom, but apart from being astonished I began to wonder what I had missed. This time there was no-one present when I made my departure, and I had a suspicion that my next lodging would be quite sober in every respect.

It was not likely to be otherwise, because my tutor had decided enough was enough and he therefore directed me to accommodation at one of Cambridge's small residential establishments for students of Theology. Amid pleasant enough surroundings, I now occupied a small and simply furnished room and lived a fairly spartan life for the rest of the academic year, but I did not join in any of the religious observances of the establishment. There were one or two other outsiders like myself, and as they kept themselves to themselves I never found out whether they had been sent for correction or had come voluntarily. Although the tranquil air of the college suited my needs, I was glad to escape from time to time to enjoy the film shows on offer at the Rex cinema, which was being managed by a young man called Leslie Halliwell, who was already making his name and was later to become a leading expert on the history of the cinema. Back at the ecclesiastical college, there were no mice in evidence and, as far as I could detect, no temptations of the flesh.

The conclusion to this unusual first year was brought about through unexpected good fortune and a burgeoning relationship that had started a year earlier. One day in Gainsborough, only a few weeks after my discharge from the sanatorium, I had met Joyce. We had known each other casually during our school days. She had thought I was too clever for her, and I had thought she was too refined for me. Our accidental meeting on the street outside the Methodist Church, of all symbolical places, immediately showed how wrong we had been and marked the beginning of something very special. My departure to Cambridge some months later strengthened rather than diminished our mutual feelings. Then, when to my surprise the Ministry of Pensions, with whom I had been in correspondence for some time regarding my medical condition, awarded me a disability pension with a substantial retrospective lump sum, I immediately asked Joyce to marry me and she agreed. By the start of my second undergraduate year we had established ourselves in a small flat, free from the ministrations of any lodging authority.

It was not difficult to resume my studies and to get involved in students' activities. As the nature of my physical limitations was a private matter, I always replied that I was useless at games whenever I was asked to join a sports club. Fortunately Norman Walters asked me to be Editor of the *Fitzwilliam House Magazine*, and this gave me a useful extra-curricular dimension. The June 1952 magazine fully reflected the tone of the times, revealing in its opening article by the Censor, W. S. Thatcher, his thoughts as Head of the House on the increasing bureaucracy which required even professors to certify in writing to the University Registry that they had resided a statutory minimum of nights. On another page Norman Walters deplored 'our Age of Utility' and said that life would be 'much more tolerable if we were to find more place for some elegance in behaviour, in graciousness and in courtesy.' I have no idea what provoked such comment. The Fitzwilliam Historical Society's report deplored the lack of students' loyalty to a cause other than their personal pursuits which had led to lack of support for a discussion on Bismarck and Lenin, to determine which had been the most evil man of the nineteenth century. More praiseworthy perhaps was the news that Fitzwilliam House in the previous November Poppy Day Appeal had collected the highest total of money in the University and had won the firkin of beer. Students, as ever, would always respond well to helping a good cause, and they would equally devote thmselves energetically to a whole range of sporting and social activities. Much of the spirit was epitomised in the lines of a sonnet written by student H. McG. Burton, which concludes:

> If you don't enjoy canasta and mix poker with gin
>   rummy,
> If you hate the thought of boxing and of writhing on
>   your tummy,
> If you idolise Mussorgsky and think Milburn plays for
>   Stoke,
> Then there's only one word for you, You're a -------
>   stupid bloke.
> There's a moral here for all to read who think this
>   poem's silly:
> 'Play up, play up, and play the game and play it for
>   Fitzbilly!'

During the next summer, more out of a need to earn a little money than from a desire to improve my teaching skills, I managed to find temporary employment for a few weeks teaching English to foreign students at a private academy in Cambridge, which many years later established itself as one of the leading providers in this field. This was sufficiently close in time to the end of the war for Britain still to be held in high esteem yet regarded with suspicion by the some of the younger students from France and Germany, of whom there were a small number to supplement the general mix of Europeans of both sexes from other countries such as Italy, Yugoslavia, Switzerland and Sweden.

I was amazed by some of the students' stereotyped views of the English, and I set out through light-hearted discussion to dispel the notion that the English cannot cook properly, that they are all hypocrites, and that they treat foreigners like idiots (which they probably do). One of my conversational practice ploys always proved successful – to consider the proposition that 'the trouble with the English is that they play cricket; the trouble with foreigners is that they don't.' The more discerning class members were able to take this at both the literal and the metaphorical levels, even if they had never played cricket in either sense. This simple experience convinced me that humour is the best weapon for breaking down national and personal barriers, especially when individual students are allowed to express themselves willingly. We experienced great friendship, and I was to meet some of the students again when they, and I, returned for more a year later. I was much indebted to the nucleus of established teachers at the school who willingly gave me good advice. Through these teaching interludes, I gained more useful experience. I also learned more about English grammar than in all my years at school – simply through having to teach it.

My encounter with students from other countries was a refreshing experience, taking me away from the insularity of my most recent academic study and reminding me of the world at large. It seemed to fit in appropriately with the decision I had already taken to switch over to the History Tripos, Part II for my third year. Once again the breadth of topics for study enabled me to make a personal selection to

109

suit my particular interests. I took readily to the reading of political theory and of modern European history, with a special study of the Revolution in France, 1848 to 1851. I was eager to have a better understanding of why nations go to war, what prevents progress in human affairs, whether we can ever achieve justice, and how we are to understand the state of the world. Lectures this year were models of excellence from Professors such as Denis Brogan, Herbert Butterfield, F. H. Hinsley and D. W. Thompson, who all shared the ability to whet one's appetite for the next weekly instalment. I particularly recall Mr Hinsley, because he was bold enough to venture into contemporary international affairs, and at that time there was a kind of unwritten law that it was not the done thing to evaluate the here and now. This, of course, was the pre-television era. Today we are inundated with instant comment. I also recall the occasion when I attended a turorial with Professor Brogan and excitedly presented what I thought was an original comment on a particular passage in Rousseau's *Social Contract*, only to be curtly acknowledged as possibly having a point.

My own supervisor of studies, Leslie Wayper, led us skilfully through our chosen routes of study and enabled me to climb to higher levels of understanding and interpretation. I felt that we shared the same radical feelings about many issues, and a year or two later when I bought a copy of his recently published book on Political Thought I was delighted to read his bold denunciation of no less than the University Vice-Chancellor for behaving as if he was 'the assured but unaccredited agent of God', when he denounced the decision by Eastern Counties Railway 'to run excursion trains to Cambridge on the Lord's Day with the object of attracting foreigners and undesirable characters to the University of Cambridge on that sacred day.' The esteem in which Leslie Wayper was held was well illustrated on 6 March 1953, the day we all heard of the death of Joseph Stalin. My first thought was to get on my bicycle and see Dr Wayper as quickly as possible, for he would have an informed view of what this event would portend for the

110

ideological struggle between East and West. By the time I arrived at his house, the door was ajar and there was a crush of students stretching from the hall into the front room. I somehow squeezed into the academic mound and listened with maximum concentration. This impromptu tutorial eventually came to an end about two hours later. We all looked forward to more the next week.

This for me was a time of great intellectual joy and of rigorous debate. When the end of year Tripos examinations took place, I was excited to find questions that suited my special interests, and despite the usual student qualms I felt I had applied myself well. When I later fought my way through the crowd to see the examination results displayed, I was overwhelmed to see that I had scored an Upper Second (Class 2 Division 1) – better than anything previously achieved. Many times subsequently I have reflected on the fact that History was the one subject that I failed in the old School Certificate examination. I am also left with the thought which I heard expressed some years later: that those who have read History do not make good civil servants, because they always see too many points of view. In my own case it was perhaps a question of being so interested in so many areas of knowledge that I never really wanted to become an out-and-out academic specialist. For this reason I was relieved when Dr Wayper advised me against doing a PhD, since by this time I had decided anyway that I wanted to do a postgraduate course of teacher training. Fortunately I was given a place on the next course at the Cambridge University of Department of Education, and it was during the next year that I was to gain a little more teaching experience prior to seeking my first full-time post.

Out of about 40 graduates in the course group to which I was assigned, there were only two or three – including myself – who expressed a desire not to teach in primary or secondary sectors. Something in me was stirring, perhaps a desire to help those who for one reason or another had not prospered at school, or older learners who wanted a second

111

chance. I was much influenced by a provocative short book by W. O. Lester Smith, *The Impact of Education On Society*, in which the author quoted Sir George Schuster, who had said: 'We cannot be satisfied with a system of education which makes those whom it influences able only to find happiness in escape from their breadwinning work . . . if the bulk of the population see their breadwinning work merely as an evil, to be reduced or escaped from as far as possible, then there must be a canker in the core of society from which a rot may spread throughout the whole.' There was an equally emotive reference to the fact that the only route to success was via the grammar school, which had historically created a deplorable social rift in secondary education. W. O. Lester Smith concluded these reflections with another argument – that we should also end the social distinction between technical college and university. So here for me was the mighty paradox of the successful grammar school boy rejecting the very system that had spawned him. However, my experience of life in the army and afterwards had already taught me that competence is not exclusively an academic quality, and not all people have had the educational opportunities they deserve.

Not surprisingly I soon found myself at loggerheads with one of my academic tutors, Bill Ingram, who was very much a product of selective education and had taught successfully in one or two prestigious independent schools. My first tutorial essay, on 'Punishment and Discipline' was beautifully typed, and I was unjustifiably pleased with it. I was less pleased when it was returned with pencilled comments written at grotesque angles on every margin of every page. I can still remember how angry I was that anyone should spoliate my writing, so angry that I failed to appreciate the logic of Bill Ingram's comments. My next essay, 'Equality of Opportunity in Education', was certain to produce another riposte – and it did: 'The whole collection of terms customarily bandied about in discussing this subject is so vague and susceptible of such vicious ambiguity that the most valuable thing one can do is to acknowledge and

112

realise this vagueness and ambiguity. That said, a great deal of the problem vanishes into what it was born of – thin air.'

However, my tutor did at least respect the final part of my essay, and here I had written as follows: 'Once equality of educational opportunity is accepted as the basis of policy, then in practice there must be an educational system which, in the first place, can cater for the needs of the whole population over as long a period of their lives as is found possible and desirable . . . Equal opportunity must ensure that children have a variety of schools including comprehensive schools, which may seem monstrous in conception to the die-hards. At the same time, equal opportunity must ensure that adults exploit the possibilities of new learning and achievement through a system of further education, which while offering further opportunities for all, also provides for the needs of those whose formal schooling was ineffective owing to retarded development or other factors.'

Mr Ingram commented: 'I could agree with your conclusion – provided you do not establish comprehensive schools without preliminary testing, or establish so many and so expensive schools that their advocates will presently say, "But you can't afford now to change back."' Mr Ingram never commented, however, on the idea of lifelong learning opportunities, although he did, later in the year, show a less dismissive attitude towards my youthful tracts.

It was thanks to him that I was placed for teaching practice at the Cambridge Technical College, where Principal Mumford was establishing an exciting reputation by introducing such liberal extra-curricular activities as music and drama, thus totally refuting the cloth-cap image of the technical student. I was fortunate in being allowed to join the choir which eventually managed a passable performance of Mozart's *Requiem Mass*, supported by the College orchestra. At the other end of the cultural scale, I was given more than my due share of gas-fitters and other day-release apprentices to whom I was required to try and teach English. It was my bad luck that on the day when I was to be assessed by a visiting tutor I had a 90-minute period with a class of apprentices. It had been a shock to discover that there is a mighty difference between wanting to help such young men and actually being able to do so, given that most of them had hated school and made very little academic progress. I cannot clearly remember what my lesson was supposed to be about, only mercifully that the apprentices paid me the compliment of at least not misbehaving. Further up the academic scale I managed to teach a few lessons to GCE classes in Literature, finding it much more difficult than I had imagined. At the end of the teacher-training year, I was deemed to have passed but without any particular merit. If I had been allowed to assess, reciprocally, the quality of some of the lectures and seminars I attended on the history of education, special subject teaching, and secondary education, I would have awarded bare passes.

Fortunately during this year, as a result of having attended a weekend training course for prospective adult education lectures, organised by the University's Extra-Mural Department, I was recruited to tutor a couple of Workers' Educational Association (WEA) evening classes in the remoter areas of Huntingdonshire. This was to prove a very practical antidote to my Postgraduate Teacher-training course. With youthful confidence I set about delivering a course on 'The English Novel' in one village and a course on 'The European Novel' in another, each to last 12 weeks. I almost completely abandoned my academic studies for the teacher-training course because of the time and effort needed to prepare two courses of lectures, many of them on authors with whose works I had little familiarity. This was my first experience of trying to teach almost from scratch. It concentrated my mind remarkably and at least enabled me to form some genuinely fresh opinions as I wrestled with ways of making the subject significant in terms of the experience and previous reading habits of my WEA students.

When you have little or no experience as a teacher, it is not always easy to anticipate what your class members will be like. If I had imagined that I would be meeting the sons and daughters of the so-called working classes for whose

114

1962. Browsing with daughter Clare

Early art work by Clare

1969. The Principal reflects

1979. H M I Business . . . Regional Staff Inspector, Dick Greenwood (right) presents the author, about to move from Lancashire to Yorkshire, with a few Manchester United souvenirs!

1987. Halton College of Further Education, Widnes, on the occasion of English Speaking Board examinations. The author with staff tutor Christine Tyler (right) and candidates

1991. H M Inspectors' reunion, Salford College of Technology. From left to right: the author, Roland Roberts and Alan Walmsley, O.B.E., who sadly died in 1993

1993. Keeping a low profile. The author and his wife, Joyce, in Corfu on holiday

1995. Old Trafford, Manchester – inside the Theatre of Dreams

enlightenment Albert Mansbridge had founded the WEA movement in 1903, I was mistaken. An early letter from one of the class organisers confirmed this: 'Most of our members are in professional employment, married, and in their 30s, and so we get either husband or wife while the other baby-sits. I am afraid that anyway, up to the present, few of our members can claim to be much like Mansbridge's "working man".' I was further informed that there had been a particularly strong branch in the village, but it had folded up after the war. However, the writer and a few others had got together to revive it (in 1953), and so far they had held two classes – one on 'Current Social Problems' and the other on 'The Progress of Political Thought'. They had apparently struggled to reach the required number of enrolments but had managed to keep the course going. The other class organiser also wrote to me before I was due to begin, explaining similar problems, plus the disquieting news that only two members had voted for the choice of subject, the English Novel, but that he had forcefully pushed for this subject. Privately he thought they were 'a dumb lot anyway'. So much for democratic administration and brotherly love!

I was relieved that one of the classes managed to keep to the required numbers, although the other had to close after only six meetings. It was a matter of domestic problems and personal priorities, irrespective of whether or not I was up to scratch. One enthusiastic pregnant lady member withdrew on health grounds. Another left because she and her husband were moving to another part of England. Then after a time I was told confidentially by the class secretary that someone had left because of his antipathy to one of the class members – something to do with a longstanding family feud. No wonder my lecture on Thomas Hardy seemed to strike a few appropriate chords, as did my account of the emergence of the eighteenth-century novelists Samuel Richardson and Henry Fielding. It was a sign of the still prudish values of post-war Britain that one of the class members said it was the first time he had ever heard a tutor use the word 'rape' – his message to me was 'Good show!' When it came a few weeks later to my talk on D. H. Lawrence, I hardly knew what to expect. (This was six years before the celebrated legal case known as The Trial of Lady Chatterley, namely Regina v. Penguin Books Limited.) On the night of my talk, a hitherto fairly taciturn middle-aged lady, whom one might have suspected, uncharitably, of the utmost prudery, suddenly leapt to the defence of Lawrence, to the astonishment of the whole class. 'He was such a wonderful man.' Not surprisingly, the class members that night enjoyed the proceedings, and went home with a few revised opinions about their fellow students.

I had no idea when I took on these commitments that such classes were subject to visits by Her Majesty's Inspectors. On the evening when a lady Inspector arrived, some of the class members seemed a little overawed by her presence, but several others were determined to have their say without let or hindrance. Realising that I was being assessed, I tried even harder than usual to keep discussion flowing after my talk on Thackeray, and I was aided by the fact that several class members had actually read much of Thackeray, especially *Vanity Fair*, and had plenty to say. The Inspector afterwards was kind enough to compliment us all, and she particularly praised the quality of the questions asked by the class members. She said to me later, when reviewing the evening's progress, 'They're not afraid to speak their minds, are they?' I was pleased and relieved that things seemed to have gone well. One class member the following week said to me, 'You were very dignified for that Inspector. Now, let's get back to your usual ribaldry.'

At the end of each course, I was required to send in a report to the regional WEA office. I said in one of my reports that I had been profoundly impressed to find a group of intelligent, eager students, the youngest 20, the oldest 70, for I had been given the impression beforehand that I was going into the backwoods. I appended written comments from the class members. One such comment was that the lectures had provoked 'considerable thought and a good deal of self-analysis'. I was particularly pleased by one

116

of the youngest members, who wrote that he had begun to find real enjoyment in classical literature, whereas at school it had seemed horridly dull. Others mentioned that they had been spurred to go on reading and to develop their own critical standards.

What I had realised for myself through this experience is the need to respect those who have not necessarily had the privilege of a higher education. Indeed, it is sometimes an advantage not to have been schooled in particular schools of thought or critical methods or attitudes. I felt it was important, too, to enjoy one's teaching and to convey that enjoyment – in contrast to some lectures I had attended where the lecturer was obviously reading from an all-too-familiar script that was boring even to its author. I had yet to learn, however, that a much more rigorous analysis and variety of teaching method would be needed to teach Literature for examination purposes. In the meantime, therefore, I was feeling full of enthusiasm and convinced that I ought to seek a post in adult education.

When an extra-mural lecturer's post at one of the Scottish universities was advertised, I immediately applied. Whether I was merely invited for interview out of curiosity, because of the fervent letter accompanying my completed form of application, or whether they simply wanted a maverick, I never found out. At the interview, my inexperience of being cross-examined was soon apparent and I was made to realise that I had not clearly thought out the distance between being one lesson ahead of one's pupils and being totally erudite, nor where I would place myself on that scale. From three sides of a large square room I received academic broadsides that totally reduced my defences, whilst grey-haired heads inclined themselves in devastating scrutiny. I was left with the conclusion that I had insufficient knowledge, as yet, and insufficient experience for the job. It was also a reflection of the tiresome conundrum so familiar to the unsuccessful candidate – you cannot get the job until you have the experience, and you cannot get the experience until you have the job.

I was not depressed for long. I knew I wanted a career as a professional teacher, and I felt I wanted to be in touch with the real world, one in which far too many people have not profited from education. My reading on education during that year had made me accept the argument that the defects of our inadequate secondary educational system needed to be remedied through better opportunities for technical and further education immediately after school. I was ready to believe that technical education and training should be delivered in such a way as to liberalise the individual and equip him to do more than simply become a wage-earner. To teach English in a technical college seemed to be one way to start, and I was pleased when I eventually found such a post in a college in the South-East. My interview this time had been before a much smaller group, and it was concentrated closely on my motives for wanting to teach in a technical college. I managed to convince the Principal and his associates on the interviewing committee that I had a genuine urge to teach English studies to a wide variety of people at many different levels and in such a way as to enrich their technical education. I had no idea of the problems that might lie ahead, but I believed that out there in the real world there was a crucial teaching job to be done.

PART 3
THE CRITICAL YEARS

We cannot afford either to fall behind in technical accomplishment or to neglect spiritual and human values.
Government White Paper on Technical Education, 1956

Rational process drives out the prophetic and the evangelical. Ministers will be less able to fly by the seat of their pants if systems thinking takes over.
Maurice Kogan, 1971

How do you persuade someone in the depths of depression that there is another way to look at his existence?
Gabriel Chanan, 1981

It is not enough to rearrange the deckchairs and to ask the band to play more loudly. It is time to start noting that people are looking for the lifeboats.
Francis Pym, 1984

Through the relatively somnolent fifties, the swinging sixties, the stressful seventies and the erupting eighties, education was a Geiger counter for growing social and political stress.

In the management of educational institutions, paternalism had begun to give way to the demand for representative and consultative modes of control – as in other professions. Teachers and lecturers found themselves caught up in the corresponding movement away from direct, didactic teaching to the arrangement of more informal, student-centred and self-directing systems of learning. Many of these teachers and lecturers were confounded by the new demands.

Throughout these years students reflected the change from relatively docile conformist youngsters into more questioning, more emancipated beings, ready to rebel even more violently against convention than any earlier generations of youth. With the return of mass unemployment, many of them felt they had been born into a no-hope society.

By the 1970s, as the need for stringent economies increased, so the movement towards the utilitarian and the practical was strengthened. Liberal elements in various curricula came to be regarded more and more as a luxury, as the education service was being directed to meet political ends. The process was merely accelerated by the rapid development of information technology and an ever-growing emphasis on management by objectives, leading later to the intrusion of methods of quality control and quality assurance.

By the 1980s, HM Inspectors, already acutely aware of the new ideas, theories and curricula affecting technical education, had also begun to feel frustrated, if not bewildered, by demands that often worked counter to what they regarded as their best traditional practice.

In all branches of the Civil Service there was equal concern – to the point where the Head of the Civil Service himself, Sir Robert Armstrong, had to reiterate to his colleagues their duty 'to impartially assist, advise and carry out the policies of the duly elected Government of the day'

and 'to give the Minister honest and impartial advice ...
whether this advice accords with the Minister's views or
not.'

The perpetual problem was to get all the interested parties
in education to agree on the best ways to meet all the needs
of the rising generation.

8

Arts and Crafts

> There can be no adequate technical education
> which is not liberal, and no liberal education which
> is not technical: that is, no education which does
> not impart both technique and intellectual vision.

A. N. Whitehead, 1932

'Sir, why do you always wear a red tie?'

Never would I as a student have dared to ask any of my
lecturers such a personal question, but this was the mid-
1950s when students were beginning to show their
individuality.

I was still learning to establish good relations with students, having realised early on that to start with I had to
find the right linguistic level, for this was the class of catering
students that had told me they could not understand all the
long words I was using. At least the question seemed a sign
of genuine interest.

'I've only got three ties, and this is the one I wear for
work.'

That was an instant and honest reply. Clothes rationing
had ended only a few years before, and I had not yet
acquired a vast wardrobe. In any case I could not afford to
buy many new clothes on my salary, despite the increments
for war service and being a four-year-trained graduate.

My student seemed satisfied, and he did not take to
wearing red ties, unlike one of his friends who, coming from

a wealthy family, had so much to spend that he made a point of wearing the same sort of expensive suits as those sported by his Head of Department, who was driven in desperation to wearing some of his older outfits. That student also learned much from the Head of Department's professional manner, and in later years became a successful hotel manager.

To many of the catering classes that I taught, anything that was not 'catering' was a complete waste of time. By the time they progressed into the second year of their City and Guilds courses, anything that I had proposed in English was met with groans of 'Oh, we did that at school.' My hopeful response of 'Ah yes, but we're going to do it DIFFER-ENTLY this time' failed to overcome their lack of enthusiasm. One particularly sullen girl student managed always to subvert anything new that I tried. Often I was nervously exhausted before I even set foot in the classroom. If I had been more experienced I would have been able to analyse the problem differently and to find a different approach. As it was I was reluctant to complain to the Head of the department, and I soldiered on. The group itself was very divided in any case into a number of small cliques, with one or two very able and academic students looking down their noses at their less learned classmates – an example of the grammar school and secondary-modern divide.

With other catering groups I was more successful, particularly in devising a series of lessons to practise customer relations in the restaurant, with the emphasis on improvised sketches in which the participants were briefed in advance on the type of roles to be played. Here students entered with gusto into the fun of being peevish clients or problem-ridden hoteliers (this was long before *Fawlty Towers* – television was only in its infancy). Some of the sketches developed were so much enjoyed that they were used in the college Christmas concert – which I was asked to organise. From this basis of learning, I was able to progress to other examples of how communication skill matters – in employment interviews and generally in personal relationships.

124

Gradually the students became receptive to the logic of practising certain types of correspondence connected with their chosen career, and later worked willingly on written projects jointly selected with their catering lecturers. It was all a question of enabling students to realise for themselves what they needed to learn and in such a way that they wanted to learn.

The problem was always to find a way to get students switched on. With day-release students, this was sometimes particularly hard, for they would take the attitude that they had left school and were sick of the classroom. They had a point, because many of the classrooms were physically unattractive, poorly furnished, and bereft of any display material. My Post-Office trainee postmen were amongst the most resentful – full of complaints about their supervisors and still shaken by their long hours of work. No-one had yet been able to convince them that they might profit from gaining a better command of language. From what little I had gathered from them, it seemed that communication at the work place was merely one-way – directed at them by an unsympathetic supervisor. One day, I suddenly decided to read them an account of a criminal raid on the sorting area of a large city post-office. The students showed immediate interest, and relished the swift and violent attack on the depot supervisory staff before the robbers escaped with a vast haul of valuables. Eventually I was able to turn their thoughts to what it would feel like to be on the receiving end of violence – and how did they think the supervisor must have felt? Their responses slowly became a little more thoughtful. It was as if we had turned round a corner into a more interesting road.

In our subsequent class sessions, conversation became a little more thoughtful as individual youngsters showed willingness to talk more naturally and honestly about themselves, their attitudes, and their interests. Eventually, each student was persuaded to give a short talk to the class on a topic of personal interest and to do this using a few guide points on preparation and presentation, and afterwards discussing individual performance. Classmates themselves were sometimes surprised to learn of one another's interests for the first time – one student spoke with authority on birds ('the sort that fly, not them with skirts'). Another was into taxidermy ('getting stuffed – ha! ha!'). A third brought an old motorcycle engine and explained he was going to overhaul it – 'it's not just a load of junk'. Everyone managed to find a personal topic on which to speak, and the immediate growth in self-confidence and clarity of speech was remarkable, yet the same class doing another subject in their day-release timetable were capable of reducing their lecturer to a state of near-hysteria through their total lack of co-operation.

There was little talk amongst staff about such problems, for reasons of self-consciousness or pride, and the idea of a more integrated syllabus with interrelated subject teaching was far away. Fortunately, the task of teaching English five times a week to full-time secretarial students was less daunting, for the initial and accepted emphasis was on the need to get a qualification in order to earn a living. At that time, in the latter years of the 1950s there were plenty of jobs to be found in commerce and industry. Students applied themselves to their tasks, and so far as English was concerned they saw the logic of improving their spelling, punctuation, grammar and general writing skills, and of learning to speak confidently and pleasantly. There were obvious correlations with other parts of the syllabus and plenty of consultation between members of staff. In my early attempts to raise writing standards, I deliberately taught sentence construction, and showed students how to progress from the simple, to the complex, and to the compound types of sentence. This was a new world to most students, and many of them actually seemed to enjoy proving to themselves that they could vary their own sentences. Later, I would put them into small groups of four or five and give them opportunities to read each other's pieces of extended writing, and to assess them on a given scale – for quality of ideas, for style, and for accuracy. On many occasions, using this approach, the students were elated that their group assessments correlated with my own. One bonus of this approach was that it taught students how to co-operate in groups and how to be mutually supportive. They all shared a desire to get the best possible results in their external Royal Society of Arts or London Chamber of Commerce examinations. Usually there were very few failures.

I encountered a completely different teaching environment teaching English as part of my timetable to a class of young teenage boys in a sanatorium just a few miles away from the college. The college Principal had received a request for someone to take on this assignment, and as he knew about my own medical history he asked if I was willing to have a go, and I agreed. When I made my first visit, the students were intrigued when I told them that I had been in their position some years before, that my own treatment (the PP) had finally come to an end in my last year at university, that I had had to meet all the medical examination requirements of the Ministry of Education in order to be passed fit to teach, that I was required to have periodical chest X-rays to confirm my continued good health, and as a bonus that I was very happily married. It was an immense relief to most of them to see that they too might get better and have a normal life, for it is particularly cruel to be struck down in adolescence and to think that you will be debarred from the opposite sex, from a career, and from the prospect of leading a normal life.

That at least, I hoped, was a boost to their morale. Then very quickly I had to start thinking what we could do together in this difficult environment. To start with, this was in the middle of a most severe Winter. The students were all bed-bound and dispersed across a long balcony exposed to the freezing air. I was dressed up like the original Michelin man, with mounds of external covering, including scarf and cap, and they were snuggled under their bed clothes, with mittens and woolly hats for added protection. Some of them had spinal tuberculosis, and so were lying flat on their backs in plaster casts. Others with pulmonary

127

disability were at least able to sit up in bed. It was going to be difficult to achieve much inter-communication, so I pushed the beds together as best I could to achieve a degree of propinquity. Everyone was in good heart, for this sort of thing was a highlight in an otherwise boring existence. After a preliminary inconclusive discussion to decide what we might do together, the boys asked me to decide.

With gentle questioning I had confirmed that they liked 'blood and thunder' stories, had a taste for the macabre, and well understood that some people will do anything to get on in life – even murder. I then explained that a man called Shakespeare had written about such things in a play called *Macbeth*, and before long we were tackling selected scenes. As enthusiasm grew, there was competition for roles, and even the poorer readers worked hard to improve their performance, despite one or two jibes from the better readers. When patients tired, I took over to explain the plot and enlarge on the text where it was of particular interest. The chaste school edition we were using had excised the more earthy parts of the Porter's remarks in Act II, so there was rapt attention when I read the unexpurgated edition. 'Cor, that's what our George says – you can't have it off proper,' said one young patient, 'if you've had a skinful of ale! "Makes him stand to, and not stand to". I like that, that's good!' At the same time, these youngsters to the best of their ability entered into sensible discussion later on when we reviewed the overall themes of the play, as well as its atmospheric effects and the immense impact that such a piece of theatre would make on the Shakespearean audience, particularly the 'groundlings' or 'tag-rag people' who, as Shakespearean scholars tell us, stood around the foot of the apron stage, nibbling nuts, drinking ale, and wenching, and roaring their responses – not unlike the standing football supporters at the old Stretford End or in the former Kop.

After three or four years at the college, I was beginning to gain in competence and experience. One day, the Principal passed on to me, for comment, a letter he had received from the local Townswomen's Guild: could the college offer a course in public speaking? I agreed to take this on, and within a short time I ran a twelve-weeks' course, with a class of about 20 women, who varied very considerably in girth and social competence, yet shared a common diffidence when required to stand up and speak. Working at first in small groups, we encouraged the skills of listening, discussing and sharing thoughts on topics of common interest to break the ice, and then moved on to short periods in which each participant had to address the group for two or three minutes. Through practice, the class members began to gain confidence and actually enjoy their position of authority. It was not long before we progressed to short formal speeches, such as introducing a meeting, or giving a vote of thanks, or proposing a toast. Later we looked more critically at the whole process of speaking and how each of us reacts to the other participants in any human situation involving people. This was the first time I had tackled such a teaching assignment with adults. It was to prove to be a continuing interest throughout the rest of my career, not that I had any idea of this when I was doing my best to help the local TWG.

There were plenty of lessons that I was also learning outside the classroom. One such lesson that I never forgot was when I made a terrible error with a GCE O-level evening class and committed the students to studying a book of poems which was no longer on that year's syllabus. All of us only realised the mistake when we saw the exam paper, after months of hard slog and expectation. I apologised as best I could to the students, most of whom were subsequently failed. On the day of the discovery, after consultation with my head of department, I reported to the Principal. He was experienced enough to realise that the examination board would not be sympathetic to this gaffe on my part, and said so. He also said that I was not the sort of person who would normally slip up and he was confident I would not repeat such a mistake. He knew, as I knew, that my own anguish was punishment enough. My colleagues were sympathetic, which helped, and I appreciated their attitude. If this had happened in my first year at the college, they might well have been inclined to be a little aloof, or even cynical, because the post to which I had been appointed had been created on the recommendation of Her Majesty's Inspectors that a graduate should be appointed for this area of work, although I was not aware of this when I joined the college.

In such a situation you learn to proceed with tact when you are probably having to supplant someone without your academic qualifications who may never have made such a mistake. In time, I felt I had done my best to work well with everyone, and indeed we were a very co-operative crowd, genuinely committed to doing our best for all the students. Inevitably, all was not sweetness and light, for there were moments when the students drove staff to despair through youthful follies such as managing to burn holes in the furniture in the students' common room. Our head of department, who was from the very nether regions north of Watford, where he assured us there was still life, habitually referred to students as 'a lot of 'herbs', though no-one worked harder on their behalf. When he left us deservedly to earn promotion in a much larger college in the west of England, we presented him with a Penguin paperback entitled *Herbs: A Manual of Herbs for the Layman, explaining the many uses to which herbs can be put*. We also gave him other more conventional gifts.

It would be an injustice to the students of that time to imply that they were irresponsible. It was in fact characteristic of the late 1950s that they were still sufficiently conformist and career-oriented to cause little real trouble. Indeed the catering students, for example, frequently won prizes at the Hotel and Catering exhibitions held at Olympia, London, and several business studies students won national prizes. I remember many charming and articulate students, who had not yet learned to challenge authority as it was to be challenged in the following decade, but they were already learning to hold their own views and to put

130

them across without offence. This was particularly true of some of the girl students from the private education sector, who would blossom rapidly in the more adult atmosphere of the college. It was interesting, too, considering the fact that students came to the college at the age of 15, that being the school leaving age, to see how quickly they matured, given the responsibility of preparing for work within a year or two.

As in many small technical colleges, most of the staff were permanent fixtures, and staff turnover was very small. The full effects of the Government's 1956 White Paper on Technical Education had yet to be realised, and the growth had yet to come. On the whole, the education provided at the college was still narrowly vocational but it seemed to suit the aspirations of so many of the students since, for one reason or another, they had not prospered at school. By degrees, and as much by accident as by design, I had begun to infiltrate more liberal elements into my teaching, such as allowing catering students to write about things other than catering, which was rather against the Principal's express wishes, or trying to encourage more reading of literature, and the development of a more critical attitude towards the popular press. I remember how it came as a shock to a group of secretarial students to discover, by analysis, just how little space was devoted to news in the most popular papers, yet they were not disposed to change their reading habits. The more determined attempts to liberalise technical education were on the horizon, and I decided to go out and look for them elsewhere. The Principal of the college was sanguine enough to advise me that in terms of career progression I ought to get into a larger college. As a true professional, he also advised me to be ambitious and climb the promotional ladder.

There is an old Chinese proverb which says that the road to success is lined with wives pushing their husbands. Suffice it to say that my wife, Joyce, fully shared the view that we should move on, and preferably to some place where we would be nearer to our respective parents. There was by now, of course, a very good reason for such thinking – the birth of our daughter Clare, whose arrival we had longingly awaited after six years of marriage. On the night when Clare was to be born I had accompanied Joyce as she was admitted into the maternity wing of the local hospital. After several unproductive hours I was sent home, for husbands at that time were not encouraged to linger in order to attend a child's birth. By the time I returned, Joyce had delivered and was looking happy, and even baby Clare seemed at ease. 'She's got a long neck like you,' were the first words addressed to me by the midwife.' Better than having a Hastings big head, I thought. Clare's expression, which I still recall clearly, was one of surprise, as if she was still stunned by the process of birth. I myself felt stunned by the sheer miracle of creation and overjoyed that we were now a proper family. Later, I cycled back to our home through the thunder and lightning which had persisted during the hours of Joyce's labour.

As Clare moved onwards into early infancy, I was lucky to be able to get home from work in time for the pleasant rituals of bedtime. In due course there was the memorable day when I was greeted with the news, as soon as I was home, 'Clare can walk!' I could hardly wait for a demonstration. My little daughter took one pace forward to demonstrate her skills to Daddy, fell over, picked herself up, and then advanced with success. Clare was already a determined child.

By the time she was two, I was appointed as a lecturer in Liberal Studies in a large regional college of art and design 'up north'. On the day we moved, our car broke down during a 250-mile journey, and it cost us a fortune to have it repaired. Once we moved into the semi-detached house we were purchasing, we found we were almost bankrupt because of the repairs needed as part of the terms and conditions of our mortgage. Clare on the very first day after we had arrived was thoroughly bewildered by this strange environment of packing cases and bare boards. We felt terrible when she burst into tears saying, 'I want to go home.' Within a day or two, having previously lived in a bungalow, she was still confused by the presence of a steep wooden stairs, as yet uncovered. Having climbed up them, she promptly fell all the way down, fortunately without serious injury. We continued to be very hard up, and just before Christmas at a secondhand book dealer we sold our set of *Chambers Encyclopaedia*, which I had been conned into buying by a very persuasive door-to-door salesman some years before. We received only about £30 – they had cost me over £100, and three years of hire purchase interest. Slowly, however, we climbed out of debt, but not before we had cleared a bank loan of £50. At this stage it seemed, for the time being, as if the pursuit of success was not a happy experience.

Making moves in one's career is always fortuitous. I was lucky at this stage, in the early 1960s, to have secured a post that was to offer constant professional stimulus. After the experience of teaching in a small technical college, where students entered at the age of 15 to take courses of one or two years' duration, I was now working with older, post-sixth-form students on Art and Design diploma courses lasting three years. The art college with its five large departments had a range of course across the whole field of fine arts, architecture and industrial design. Its spacious exhibition gallery was constantly showing either students' work or examples of art and sculpture by notable contemporary artists and designers. In the course of regular visits to all parts of the college to liaise with the art and design staff, I saw the students at work on their own specialisms and began to enlarge my own knowledge of how they were being taught and encouraged to develop their individual creativity. Once I had become used to seeing nude models posing for life-drawing sessions, my attention turned to noticing how individual students varied in their concentration, organisation and personal appearance. It was interesting also to work out how the individual Art and

133

Design tutors fulfilled their professional roles – varying between gentle encouragement and cruel comment, and between formal supervision and informal presence.

It was becoming increasingly recognised officially, in all post-school courses, whether in regional colleges, colleges of technology, or technical colleges, that students should have the opportunity to undertake some sort of General or Liberal Studies during their specialised course for entry into the various professions. The aims of such studies had been frequently defined – to educate the specialist, to liberalise the individual, to enable the student to learn something of human values. I had quickly discovered in my new post that higher education in the art world does not automatically produce liberal-minded and cultured graduates in Art and Design. The college employing me had already recognised the problem by introducing elements of academic study some years before – Literature, Philosophy, Classical Studies. The time had now come to devise a more ambitious programme of 'complementary' studies, with compulsory elements for all courses.

Our thinking was much influenced by the practice of one of the newer universities, Keele, which had introduced a completely new first year of course studies covering general educational and academic themes. Partly adopting this approach but also tailoring our provision to the academic capabilities of lecturing staff, we were able to give students a weekly dose of lectures and tutorials on themes such as 'Man in Modern Society', covering religion, politics, social issues and the mass media, followed in the second year by a look at 'The Arts Today'. Gradually in the course of time the lectures by the Art and Design staff on the History of Art were linked whenever possible to the complementary studies. One of the most successful ploys, illustrating the need for an integrated approach to course work, was to bring together individual lecturers and heads of department from the specialist Art and Design staff, enabling them to take part in seminars on more general themes relating to the role of the artist or designer in society.

134

While it is difficult to assess contemporary events and issues with complete impartiality, no-one denied the validity of making the attempt. Most students themselves were keen to understand what forces were operating around them, for this was a time of declining belief, of the realisation that God, King and country as ideals were being supplanted by growing materialism and the belief that 'you never had it so good', as claimed by Conservative Prime Minister Harold Macmillan. The job of the Liberal or Complementary Studies lecturer was to try and present the facts impartially, so that students could make up their own minds. One colleague of mine was so successful when he gave a lecture on Christianity that whereas one group of students thought he was 'a bloody atheist', another group dismissed him as 'a God-botherer', a term which had originated in the Royal Air Force to describe over-zealous Padres. Students were equally divided when it came to the discussion of brainwashing, as experienced by captured American pilots during the Korean war in the early 1950s, and of deciding what degree of coercive persuasion each student might withstand and for what worthwhile causes.

It would be an exaggeration to assume that all students enjoyed their Complementary Studies, for such elements in the course could be seen as too thoroughly bourgeois or too supportive of the Establishment. Some students therefore instinctively identified with those contemporary writers, such as John Osborne, John Braine, or Kingsley Amis, who were dubbed 'angry young men' for the way they expressed their discontent with the cultural and political mood of the times. The early 1960s saw the growth of the Campaign for Nuclear Disarmament (CND) and the explosion by the Russians of the biggest ever megaton bomb. The horrific prospect of international conflict and Armageddon was suddenly experienced in 1962 during the Cuban missile crisis, when the Russians managed to assemble nuclear missiles in Cuba with the potential to wipe out 80,000,000 Americans. How that crisis was overcome is one of the more fascinating tales of contemporary history. Its effect at the

135

time on the students I taught was that on the most critical night of the crisis, when everyone really feared that an atomic war was only hours away, many of these young men and women sought consolation through sex, especially those who were still virgins. This was hardly the sort of matter that all students would openly discuss after the crisis, though some did, and there were plenty of similar reports from other educational establishments. As some of us had indicated in our earlier course lectures, people cannot accurately predict how they will behave in the direst situations. Now the students had experienced their first dose of real stress.

Other students genuinely enjoyed their complementary studies, particularly those who recognised the need to become articulate not just through their own art or design work but through their command of language as well. This was often more the case with Design students than with those immersed in fine art, since their field of work was more naturally a matter of learning to produce and sell items for a mass market – whether in terms of textile design or graphic design. Many of them were willing to believe that how you speak is a matter of importance, for television had not yet accustomed us to the sloppy standards of articulation prevailing in the 1990s, and so in the 1960s art and design students were still inclined to argue fiercely as to whether accent matters. On one occasion, a young woman student sought my advice: she came from Oldham and said that other students laughed at her accent. She spoke clearly and with an extensive vocabulary, and I told her this. We agreed that she should set out to excel in her art work, which she did, and I told her to ignore silly comments from others, and she did. The problem disappeared. On another occasion, with a receptive group of students, I was drawn into trying to illustrate different varieties of regional accent, including the kind of Lincolnshire accent that I spoke as a child. 'Why don't you speak like that all the time?' they asked, after my attempt to sound like Tennyson, the Lincolnshire poet.

All this was part of a deliberate attempt to promote social

awareness, the gaining of which is not without pains for the young. At that particular period in the early 1960s, educational institutions were still able to shape their own Liberal or Complementary Studies programmes without too much external *diktat*. My own experience at that time had led me to believe that if you try to relate Complementary Studies entirely to Art and Design, you become obsessive, and equally if you deliberately avoid any relationship you may fall into useless academicism. We had found that there are times when students welcomed study that is utterly unconnected with their main course work. The Summerson Council, one of the officially appointed bodies to pronounce on art education, had declared in 1962 that 'we are fundamentally concerned with the development of attitudes rather than with the presentation of facts'. However, subsequent reports on art education were to make people more preoccupied with the question of subject matter than with the values that ought to underlie the whole educational process, and pressure increased to intensify the time given to teaching the History of Art, at the expense of broader Complementary Studies programmes. As institutions and courses expanded, the sheer practicalities of timetabling made it less easy to release whole blocks of students simultaneously from across several departments, a past strategy that had enabled students of different disciplines to come together and escape their own intensive specialisms, so that the Graphic Design student could argue with the budding sculptor about contemporary issues. Subsequent developments in post-school education were to drive the curriculum into narrower channels.

It was still possible to argue at this time, with real conviction, that there is not a permanently ideal content either in Complementary Studies or in Art and Design education generally. The view I had arrived at is that you should set out to recruit competent staff with wide interests and acceptable professional qualifications, so that they find the formula that is appropriate to the needs of a particular college, as well as to the climate of educational thought.

Thus there could be valuable permutations, but differing ones – not one unique and binding solution. It was important too, to use the staff of all departments in such a way that they contributed to something more than mere training, for as the political economist John Stuart Mills had said in the nineteenth century: 'Men are men before they are lawyers, physicians, or manufacturers. If you make them capable and sensible men, they will make themselves capable and sensible lawyers, physicians, lawyers and manufacturers.' It seemed to me that this sentiment was still relevant in the 1960s. It certainly became one of my stock quotations.

My experience of teaching Art and Design students had done much to enlarge my own intellectual horizons, for I had quickly had to familiarise myself not only with the specialist skills being encouraged in Art and Design courses, but with the full range of social, political and economic developments affecting our post-war society, since these were the subjects of many of our Complementary Studies lectures. As I had discovered when I myself was a student, the hardest subject to comment on with wisdom is that which is happening now, but it seemed a very legitimate task to try and help all these young people to understand the complex forces that would be governing their future lives and to increase their capacity to make their own independent judgments. These were laudable objectives, even if one had no certain way of knowing if one was achieving them, and they presented a great challenge to tutors and to students at all levels. This was especially true of the less privileged part-time day-release students, in whom I had developed a special interest – in this case, painting and decorating apprentices for whom a dose of Liberal Studies was timetabled for one hour at the end of a very long day at the college. I was to enlarge my learning thanks to them.

With the co-operation of the caretaker of the separate premises in which they were taught, I was able to arrange for them to have a cup of tea before we commenced proceedings. This saved them having to queue in the college

138

refectory at that time, and gave them less reason to arrive ten minutes late. It also broke the ice and enabled a little informal chat to take place before the Liberal Studies began. The young men quickly showed a willingness to behave less disruptively than I had feared, and before long became receptive to learning something about the years of the Second World War and its aftermath, which they were still anxious to understand more clearly, having been born two or three years after 1945. I soon found myself trying to explain it all in clear and meaningful terms, and this led on to later quite civilised sessions. During this period, the apprentices gladly gave me some practical tips on home decorating, especially how to use wet and dry rubbing on paintwork, or how to prepare walls prior to applying wallpaper. At home, I improved my painting techniques, but the first time I tried to paper a ceiling, the first length of pasted paper fell off the ceiling when I was half-way across the room, and it ended up mangled and defunct. That taught me not to undervalue manual skill.

In my own professional work, I had learned much on the art of negotiating and persuading, since one of my main tasks had been to go around the college and talk to heads of department and senior staff about the Complementary Studies programme and the possible times at which it could be delivered. As with students, so with members of staff – there were considerable variations of attitude. Some heads of department were more inflexible than others, for so much depended on the need to use studio accommodation to maximum capacity, which could not be achieved within their existing system if large numbers had to be away for as much as half a day, added to which was the effect on their own staff and course timetabling. After five years of this type of diplomatic activity, I had won a few battles, lost as many, and earned much friendship. I was pleased one year to accept an invitation to sit on one of the staff panels interviewing potential students, and for the first time I witnessed an overseas candidate applying for a course in textile design, who produced his wallet at a crucial point in the interview and meaningfully said that his father, who was a very rich man, would be very disappointed if his son was not admitted to the college. Fortunately, the head of department conducting the interview was not unused to such situations. He had already noticed that this candidate's written application bore a striking resemblance to an earlier application from a now unsuccessful student. Some educated village scribe in a distant land was making a fortune. Our head of department maintained his integrity, even to the point of genuinely counselling the dubious candidate on more honourable educational alternatives.

I was fortunate both in this post and in my previous one that I too had received some useful counselling. In my first post the Principal had raised my morale considerably just before I left by giving me his optimistic view of my career prospects. I was not convinced of his opinion that I too might eventually become a college Principal, because I thought one needed a technical degree for such elevation. Now, after several more years of experience, I was more optimistic because the Ministry of Education seemed to be attaching great importance to general educational values in technical education. In addition, I had by now become involved at regional and national levels in several courses for Liberal Studies teachers. Then I had a rather encouraging conversation with my present Principal, who had no doubts that I should begin to look for a more senior post elsewhere, so if a Principalship of a small college was advertised I should apply, with his full support.

I began to watch the educational press.

9

In the Hot Seat

One Principal delegated nearly everything and, because a measure of control was missing, appeared to be sometimes out of touch with what was going on in the college. Another Principal, on the other hand, tried personally to attend to nearly all matters of detail and was having a hard job to cope with the administrative load of an expanding college. Clearly the Principals needed to be aware of the dangers of these extremes and to seek a sensible compromise.

D. Charlton *et al*
The Administration of Technical Colleges, 1971

My elation as I drove to my first interview had turned into panic as I found myself stuck in a traffic jam, still ten miles from my destination. I eventually reached the college with only seven minutes to spare before my specified arrival time. There were no other candidates in the waiting room into which I was pointed, after the briefest of verbal exchanges. I was just trying to anticipate the next move and to scan one or two notes I had made about the college, when I was suddenly summoned into the interview room.

I gave what I thought was a courteous smile before replying as best I could to the initial conventional questions, gradually realising that hardly any of the 12 or so panel members was bothering to make any direct eye-contact, or to convey any warmth or encouragement. I quickly suspected that I had only been invited to make up the required number for the shortlist, for I was being given no opportunity to put across all those key points that I had previously worked out in my favour. Quite to the contrary, the drift of some of the later questions was to suggest that I was probably not suited to this particular post, since I was not a specialist in Business Studies, that being the area of course provision in which the panel seemed most interested.

By the time the interviews had been completed, I had at last encountered the other four candidates, who all seemed reluctant to talk much about their own experience with the panel or to express any surprise that we had not yet met the Principal of the college. After the panel had made its choice of candidate, those of us who were unsuccessful congratulated the winner and wished him all the best. With his considerable experience as head of a large Business Studies department, he would no doubt do a good job as Principal. I suspected that in many ways he knew a great deal more about this college than I did.

In fact, I had a feeling as I drove home that there was something rather odd about this whole appointment process. It was almost an unconscious demonstration of how not to arrange interview proceedings, since there had been no opportunity to ask anyone any questions of any significance before the interview, and only the briefest time to tour the college. Shortly afterwards, I learned to my surprise why we had not been able to see the Principal – he was in custody awaiting trial for having helped himself to a considerable slice of college funds. A subsequent prison sentence ended his academic career. From further reports, it seemed that it was a matter of domestic difficulties that had led to his downfall. It was not clear whether his domestic problems were caused by his professional commitments. The college had done well to keep the matter concealed for so long.

I tried not to feel over-optimistic when I applied for another Principalship some weeks later, but was pleased in due course to be invited for interview. This time a whole morning was programmed to enable the candidates to visit the college and its two main departments – Engineering and General Studies – and to have a pleasant, informal conversation with the Principal, who was due to leave for the Principalship of a much larger college. One or two of the other candidates had also been interviewed with me at the Business Studies college, and we shared a few amicable thoughts and wished one another better luck this time. It demanded great artifice to appear charming when you really hoped they would not do well. The hypocrisies continued during the afternoon, when we were all together at the town hall awaiting interview by a large municipal committee. The first three candidates looked quite disconsolate as they emerged in succession from the interviews. I was next to go in, so I made myself breathe slowly and deeply. It seemed to make no difference.

On this occasion, there was nothing odd about the conduct of the interview. I was able to speak with conviction about education, the role of the local college, vocational training, and the needs of young people in answer to the various leads I was given. As I came out of the interview, I felt it had gone as well as I had dared to hope. Then followed a long wait, with two more candidates being interviewed, and about 40 minutes of deliberation after that. All sorts of hopes and fears were going through my mind. At last the final moment came: it was my name that was called out. I returned to the interview room and formally accepted the post that was now offered. When I returned to the waiting room, the other candidates had gone. A few minutes later, amid the levelling environment of the gentlemen's room, the Chairman of the governors, having also emptied his bladder against the opulent porcelain stalls, reminded me that I would be welcome any time at the Labour Club.

This was early in 1964, and in the following autumn a Labour government was elected. The political climate of the day favoured the expansion of technical education and the growth of day release, not only for apprentices in industry but for young workers in other occupations who might profit from special courses of general education not necessarily connected with their vocation. It was into a college endeavouring to meet these objectives that I was plunged a few weeks later, carrying the good wishes of many professional friends and colleagues who regarded my appointment as a boost to teachers of Liberal Studies. One former colleague, with many years of service in further education behind her, warned me that the post of Principal would have its rough side as well as its smooth. I was one of the youngest college Principals in the country, full of optimism, and not inclined to believe her.

Amid the excitement of my appointment I had never really stopped to ask what sort of skills were needed to do the job. I carried a rather naive remembrance of headmasters who always seemed invincible and proficient, and in recent years of two college Principals whose entirely different management styles I had begun to notice while I had been under their command. One had been a model bureaucrat in the best sense, conditioning his staff to working through channels; the other had governed with more panache, encouraging spontaneity and informal lines of communication and control. The concept of command was largely accepted by ex-servicemen like myself, no matter what the style was, but as the swinging sixties gained momentum there was to be a more open challenge to authority, not only by adolescents but also by employees – and this was true of technical teachers as their unions began to flex their muscles. Therefore I should not have been surprised on my first day in the Principal's office when I came face to face with a deputation of angry lecturers who were considerably worked up by the prospect of an extended working year of 48 instead of 36 working weeks. I had never before heard any technical lecturers so worked up, and I was unsure as to why this issue had suddenly come to a head. It was a matter of listening patiently, before convincing them that the matter would be thoroughly aired in due course after consultation with all the parties involved.

The matter was subsequently resolved after a series of meetings.

This episode quickly persuaded me to review the methods of staff consultation in the college in terms of both formal and informal meetings. The college had grown in the last year or two to a point where it was no longer possible to manage the college by relying on the mid-morning coffee break as the main means of communication, yet with a staff of only 50 lecturers it would have been absurd to have a profusion of official committees. What was important at that stage of college development was to ensure that every member of staff, full-time or part-time, had access by right to the head of department and to myself. However, my experience made me realise that people need time to accustom themselves to a new leader. I had to feel my way carefully at a time when the teaching unions were spurring on staff in their battle for better conditions of service and a more participative role in college affairs.

What members of staff seldom realised was the extent to which the college was controlled by the local authority, though the more militant lecturers sometimes sent their various complaints directly to the Chief Education Officer, merely to be told what I, as the servant of the authority, had already explained to them. It was then a matter of interpretation on their part as to whether I was acting in good faith, or merely conspiring to thwart them. The rank and file members of staff had no idea that the college Principal met regularly with the Principals of the authority's other colleges preparing to challenge the authority's financial provision and further education policy. Equally they would not know that the Chief Education Officer would be fighting his own battle with the town hall to get better budgetary allowances. Thus it was not easy amid all these separate conflicts to make staff see the common ground and to work together for what was, after all, the real purpose of the college – to provide education and training for its students.

I quickly realised that there was great potential for achievement in the college both by students and staff, and that engagement in worthwhile enterprise quickly broke down barriers and created goodwill. I therefore welcomed approaches by my colleagues to get students involved in helping a nearby school for handicapped children. As a result, a group of engineering apprentices designed and built a battery-driven kiddicar for one of the most severely handicapped pupils. Another group of students arranged a football match in which the more able pupils played against a team of college students. The referee ruled out every student goal as offside and awarded enough penalties to the school side to enable them to win comfortably. This was not seen as patronising but merely as well-intentioned. That was what I said to my doctor when I had to visit him for treatment to torn ligaments incurred by own participation in the match. I had lasted only two minutes before falling heavily. My doctor thought I had been very foolish. Fortunately I earned much sympathy from college staff and felt I was becoming accepted.

With my particular interest in day-release students, I devised a questionnaire which was completed by 300 apprentices to express their feelings and attitudes about work and college. The replies were given anonymously and without restraint. The section on 'my relations with college staff' contained the following comments:

'I have respect for the staff, but I think I have put away the "Yes Sir, No Sir" attitude I had at school.'

'Relations slightly strained at the moment because of the cock-eyed way them (sic) reports are filled in.'

The response to 'what my employer thinks about day release' included:

'It does him as much good. He knows an educated person benefits him.'

146

'He doesn't like day release but he lets us go so the firm won't get a bad name.'

The one answer that shook me, in the final general section inviting free comment, was:

'THE PRINCIPAL IS NON-EXISTENT.'

So, no matter what I tried I could not be personally known to every part-time student, but the important thing was to find ways of making all students feel they were treated as human beings, not as mere enrolment statistics. I was particularly encouraged by the efforts of my colleagues to treat apprentices as adults and to help them develop their talents – legitimately of course, for an engineering workshop could always be used for the occasional illicit purpose, such as the manufacture of metal washers that would fool the refectory vending machines into supplying tea or coffee.

With the full-time students, there were inevitably better opportunities to develop honest talent. I had decided to keep my hand in with teaching, and therefore took on a group of full-time GCE students once a week in order to encourage their skills in speaking and negotiating. We agreed upon an outside project, which took them to a nearby housing estate to question householders about their views on capital punishment, especially hanging. They devised a simple questionnaire to indicate the different shades of opinion, and working in pairs with official letters of identification from the college they obtained the necessary responses. Their experiences were quite instructive – some were mistaken for the television programme 'Candid Camera' and received no help; many were told in no uncertain terms to ... off; but more than half the tenants, after initial suspicion, gave a helpful reply. Most students had never before had such an assignment and returned to college full of personal anecdotes to share with the class. Later that year, 1965, a motion for the abolition of capital punishment was approved in Parliament after a long passage through both Houses. The decision was only just consistent with the results of the students' survey.

At this period in further education, the emphasis was very much upon the need to develop general skills as well as technical or vocational expertise. There were many training officers in local industry who supported a broader approach to engineering courses, and they were frequent visitors to the college, as were Her Majesty's Inspectors, who constantly encouraged the introduction of general educational elements in the training curriculum and took careful note of all that was going on in the college. It was heartening to feel that, despite problems of finance and accommodation, we were making genuine attempts to offer students, whether full-time or part-time, an educational experience that would prepare them for their future lives and responsibilities. This period was also one of great flux, for the school leaving age was due to be raised within a few years to 16, and this was already causing colleges and schools to re-think their courses and curricula. When I spoke at a conference in Wales about such matters and stressed the value of a liberal approach, I received a rather depressing response from several members along the lines of 'It's OK for you, you're a Principal who believes in all this. What can we do in a college with a Principal who does not share your philosophy?' My reply, I fear, was not very reassuring, though I tried to suggest they should not give up the fight.

By this time, I was beginning to believe that there was a real battle to be waged and that I would like to fight it on an even bigger front. Strangely enough, on the night I arrived home from Wales, a former colleague now employed in a larger college in the next county telephoned me to say that the Principal of her college had just announced his intention to retire. She thought I would like to know this, and she was right. So shortly afterwards I was ready with my application when the advertisement appeared in the educational press for the Principalship of this larger establishment. It seemed an opportunity not to be missed, and in practical terms if I were selected for the post I would not need to move house, since the college was within tolerable commuting distance, and my daughter Clare could continue at the same school. Then I began to wonder how, in the event of success, I could withstand any charges of disloyalty, for my departure from my present post would perhaps be seen as unexpected and somewhat premature after only three years. However, the prospect of being head of a much larger college became a fixation, which fortunately was acceptable to my family. Now it was a matter of waiting daily for the postman to arrive.

Just over a month later, by which time I was beginning to give up hope, I received an invitation for interview over two successive days, the first for a visit to the college and the second for a formal interview. The tour of the college was much as I expected, with all five candidates keeping a low profile. Three of us were college Principals from different parts of the country, so the competition was going to be keen. The other two were departmental heads. On the next day, my interview by a large committee of college governors progressed pleasantly. Soon after it began, and just as I was warming up in the middle of an impassioned statement about further education, one of the governors asked me out of the blue whether I believed it was correct to split an infinitive. When I replied that 'to NEEDLESSLY split an infinitive is a crime', the questionner smiled with satisfaction and said no more. Fortunately for me I had been forewarned by one of the governors, to whom I was known through previous professional contacts, that such an odd question might crop up. It was merely a slight hiatus in the proceedings, after which the Chairman of Governors quickly moved the proceedings on. Towards the end of the interview, just when I was beginning to feel that things had gone well – some smiling faces and nodding heads following some of my responses – a rather aggressive looking governor pointed to a small gap in my CV. 'What were you doing that year?' My memory failed me, and I had to reply as politely as possible that I just could not remember. Someone then who must

149

have wanted to support me immediately said, 'Well, I'm sure you weren't sewing mailbags, were you?' I instantly agreed. There were no further awkward moments.

As soon as my interview was over, I was pointed in the direction of another room, this time away from the other candidates. I was rather worked up, though relieved to have finished, and scarcely noticed my surroundings, which eventually struck me as rather cramped – a sort of converted broom cupboard. Some considerable time later, I thought I heard voices, and in fact I was sure someone was calling my name. Within a minute or two I was located by a very surprised official who explained that I should have gone to the third room on the right, which was a waiting room, and not to the first door, which had indeed led me into a small store room; but of more importance was his invitation that I should return to the interview room, where I was formally offered the post and accepted it.

Some months later, as Principal of this larger college, I was immediately aware that I was now working for a much more competitive education authority. Compared to what I had been accustomed to, the scale of expenditure was lavish, as the Governors strove to keep the college to the fore in its further education and training provision, and the officers of the new authority encouraged their Principals to push ahead with college development. Several college Governors visited the college regularly to see its work and to discuss educational issues, links with industry, and co-operation with local schools. Many of these Governors held senior professional posts in industry and commerce, and keenly supported the idea of the college working outwards to promote education for students of all ages. The authority's subject advisers were also in constant touch with myself and the college staff, and kept a very close eye on my activities during my first term. Our relationships were very amicable and based on genuine mutual trust. Consequently an effective system of checks and balances developed, so that the proposals put to the Governors' meetings were usually realistic, since they were the result of prior discussion, and

150

most of the agenda items were approved without difficulty at that stage, in the hope of further approval from the education committee. It was only occasionally, for example at the December meeting just before the agenda was due to be concluded in anticipation of a sumptuous Christmas lunch, and Governors were looking impatiently at the clock, that one or two more extravagant items of expenditure were rushed through.

Working on a larger scale than in my previous post meant finding more efficient and effective ways of managing college affairs, especially as the total staff numbers began to increase to meet the expansion of courses. This was still a time when the tradition of autocratic rule held sway, but my own instinct was towards participative management and open lines of communication, especially through departmental heads, whom I met individually and collectively on a regular basis, so that our role as a management team was consolidated. All key decisions were officially presented to all college staff by means of a regular Principal's bulletin, and full staff meetings were held at appropriate intervals, usually the beginning and end of term. Special efforts were made to ensure that part-time staff were kept informed of college developments, and they were encouraged to liaise with full-time staff. Such procedures were not remarkable, but for some members of staff they were an innovation after years of quiet individual isolation. A further ploy that generated positive support was to hold an end-of-year staff conference to discuss college policy and educational developments in general, using outside speakers as well as college staff. At the end of my first year in office, I organised this myself; the second year it was arranged by departmental heads; and the third year it was delivered by the staff association on behalf of all teaching and non-teaching staff. The tradition then continued, and provided a useful focus for discussing various proposals for major changes in the control of colleges through the creation of bigger governing bodies and of the so-called Academic Boards by the Department of Education and Science.

The Department was also beginning to draw attention to the need for more staff of technical colleges to have a teacher training qualification. My response to this was to send as many untrained staff as possible on part-time training courses, but the necessary preliminary to this was to introduce a system of staff development, starting off with each member of staff having an informal interview with myself so that all individual professional needs could be discussed. This was a particularly time-consuming procedure but it paid dividends, especially for those older members of staff who felt they had been left to languish. They now welcomed the new interest in their professional work and progress. All these assessments were related effectively to the question of upgrading and promotion within the college establishment, and it gave staff a better incentive to apply to attend national, regional and local courses and conferences designed to extend their professional knowledge and skills. A similar system of staff appraisal was introduced for non-teaching staff, producing mixed reactions as maintenance staff feared that the introduction of an 'organisation and methods' approach would lead to loss of jobs, but the fears proved unfounded. All in all, it was my belief that we needed to give staff the best possible opportunities and training to provide the best possible courses for students. Inevitably, there were financial limits to be observed, but the college Governors and the Local Education Authority shared my belief in staff development and training, and expenditure estimates for this heading were usually approved without alteration.

It was one thing to aim at having a fully trained teaching staff, but in deciding priorities one always had to ask: what should the college be providing? Historically the answer was more of the same, the assumption being that the demand would continue for traditional technical courses. However, as individual college aspirations grew, the competition between institutions became more apparent, as did the rivalry to cater for students when they reach the age of 16. With the support of the Education Authority, I worked with colleagues to develop good relations with local schools and to discuss the future needs of school leavers. The problem was to avoid charges that the college was merely trying to steal all school pupils. I felt that some proper form of review of post-16 provision would eventually have to be undertaken by the Education Authority. In the meantime, several invitation conferences with head teachers were held, and an excellent college catering department lunch was always provided and appreciatively consumed, but the time was not yet ripe for head teachers to start giving ground. As one headmistress wrote to say, 'it was a pity that they could not see the beginnings of a collaborative scheme in the attempts you made to draw the college and the secondary schools together when you took up your appointment three years ago.'

As the 1960s slipped away, there were other interesting developments, not the least being the influx of more and more students from overseas, who were required to pay high fees and therefore brought in more income. I found it hard to accept this policy when there were still so many UK students who needed further education, but for the time being it was not too big a problem as many overseas students were applying for higher, not further, education. Larger institutions than ours with advanced work began to exploit this opportunity.

Then again, there was a growing demand from mature students, particularly older adults who wanted to return to learning, and as this area of work expanded it led to the establishment of a further college department, which in turn found itself at loggerheads with the Adult Education courses network based in local evening centres. Here again, it was difficult to avoid charges of poaching students, since the college increasingly attracted adult students because of its better facilities. In fact it was the same problem in every course area, for example in Engineering as the demand for more industrial training increased. Soon there was increased conflict with other technical colleges within the broader region and a growing feeling that everything was becoming a free-for-all. Our heads of department meetings became more difficult as we all faced the problem of growing rivalries and competition with other institutions. We knew that if you make a provision to meet a demand for courses, the demand increases if you do the job well. On top of that, if you make a provision for something NEW, that too will stimulate a demand, provided you are offering a quality course. So all the time there was a need to find an equilibrium, given the traditional provision, the new initiative provision, the existence of other competitors, the constraints of local authority funding, the monitoring by the Regional Advisory Council for Further Education, and the imposition of government policy through the advice and instructions of the Department of Education and Science and Her Majesty's Inspectorate.

Despite all these administrative networks and the pressure to keep abreast of educational development, it was always a priority to have an effective tutorial system so that students could be guided not only in their courses but in their personal affairs. My own feelings, which I conveyed to staff, were that most people will do most things in reason, provided you let them know clearly that what you want them to do is in their own interests. College lecturers nominated as class tutors were therefore encouraged to talk to students individually, to take an interest in their career prospects, to steer them into Students' Union activities, and to make them think constructively about their behaviour and their attitudes to other people. At this particular period, College of Further Education students had not yet gained complete financial autonomy, and any cheque issued for a major item of expenditure had to be signed by a designated member of staff as well as by the students' union treasurer. This was a mutually accepted constraint at a time when students were becoming much more assertive about their rights. Their search for more autonomy was perhaps a faint echo of the attitudes of their elder students in universities such as the Sorbonne, or Oxford, where students in the late 1960s indulged in rioting. My own young students, aged 15

154

upwards, were reacting energetically to the growing pop culture, and held a series of quite spectacular discos. Unfortunately, in their exuberance to have an even bigger and better 'gig', they committed themselves by signing a contract to hire a very expensive national pop group before they considered the economics of the venture. The tickets for the event were so expensive that an insufficient number was sold, but when the students then tried to cancel the event they were held to the contract and had to pay the agreed fee. It was so huge that it wiped out all that year's Students' Union funds. Somehow one or two subsidies were arranged to help them out. The students learned much from this episode.

Another example of students learning through experience how to restore their own reputation occurred when some angry local residents complained about the amount of litter being deposited by students in the roads by the college. This was turned into a system whereby any local resident with a legitimate complaint was encouraged to telephone the Students' Union, and immediate action would be taken not only to clear the litter but to identify the litterbugs if possible and get them to apologise. On one particular occasion, when a group of students were accused of vandalising an old lady's front garden, the students on the same day replanted her front garden and presented her with a bouquet of flowers. What was important in this system of meeting complaints was to have both full-time and part-time students in the action groups. The system worked well during my time at the college, not only in reducing litter spreading but also in deterring student motorcyclists from dangerous driving. Eventually, the college set up a Residents' Committee, comprising students, staff, and local residents, and this monitored progress. However, there was always a need for vigilance and prompt action.

One of the most successful and positive student initiatives occurred one year, when just before Christmas the Students' Union put on a Christmas tea party for visitors from a local children's home. The students provided everything – transport to and from the college; plenty of children's fare; presents; and entertainment by novitiate student magicians and clowns. One Business Studies full-time student, who was normally rather withdrawn and not a little unco-operative, amazed his tutors by the energy and enthusiasm with which he joined in the proceedings. His sudden acclaim led to a much improved academic performance the next term.

There were always other stories of student success, many of them demonstrating that some youngsters responded better in the more adult atmosphere of a college than in the regime of school. That is not to denigrate the school, nor to praise the college, merely to record that some head teachers were glad to see the back of certain pupils. It was not uncommon for some of these youngsters, after completing their college courses, to write to their former head teachers to let them know how well they had done in their GCE examinations. It was all a question of the particular conditions in which certain types of student will flourish, as well as the stage they happen to be at in the path to maturity.

At the other extreme, a rather unusual example of a problem student occurred one summer, beginning with an unexpected visit to the college by a rather distraught professional gentleman who gained access to my office after prolonged negotiation with my secretary. He turned out to be the manager of a large bank, at which one of our overseas students had an account. Unfortunately, unbeknown to all of us at the college, our student was running up huge gambling debts in a casino and expecting to have a limitless bank overdraft. This was a matter of acute embarrassment to the bank manager, because the student's father was a wealthy entrepreneur whose financial dealings were of considerable importance to the bank, and the bank manager and upper echelons did not want to cause any embarrassment to the father. The bank manager was clearly in a quandary. We agreed to accept the challenge.

We interviewed the student cautiously, a week later, by which time his intermittent absences from college had been noted with interest and used as a pretext for a confrontation by myself and his head of department. The young man had taken a few days off before Christmas, informing his course tutor that he urgently needed to meet his father, who was making an unexpected visit to this country. However, through contact with the student's bank manager, we had confirmed that the father had not been to this country at all. When we confronted the student with our knowledge that his excuse for his last absence was a complete lie, he was not at all surprised and remained totally calm. He was then told that unless he improved his ways, he would be expelled through failure to observe his obligations as a student. We were still watching the situation closely when, two weeks later, the student left the college. We never found out whether the bank manager's neurosis continued, or whether the student was brought to task by his father.

Incidents like these brought minor elements of drama into my professional life. By coincidence, at that time I came across a statement by a psychologist who said that organisations need elements of three things – routine, ritual, and drama. Routine, the daily round of activity, gives people a feeling of security and confidence, though it may diminish their capacity to look critically at what they do. Ritual, as expressed through formal establishment ceremonies such as prize givings or periodical assemblies for one purpose or another, helps to sanctify the establishment. Drama, meaning the unexpected event that calls on people's often unknown resources, may give organisations a challenge they would not willingly seek. Quite unexpectedly, towards the end of the 1960s we had a series of hoax bomb alerts which through their unfortunate regularity began to relate to all three of the psychologist's elements. Clear procedures were carefully worked out for such a contingency, in collaboration with the local police and the fire services, firstly to decide if the alert was likely to be genuine and secondly to ensure that everyone knew exactly how to get out of the building as quickly as possible. The disruption on these occasions was severe and the annoyance gargantuan, especially on a

157

cold, dark November afternoon when hundreds of people had to assemble in the grounds of the college and instant roll calls had to be taken. Eventually, the police apprehended the culprits, who were local schoolboys. We were not inclined to let them enrol at the college when they left school.

After this trauma, and as further time elapsed, I was beginning to wish that I had inexhaustible wisdom, wit, compassion, psychological insight, and energy. At least I was fortunate to have supportive senior colleagues who were prepared to work with me as a team and to learn with me through experience. Often I would be led into useful reflection after a quite casual remark or incident, such as when a head of department asked me if I consciously set out to appoint staff with similar qualifications and experience to my own. That question subsequently led me to search for variety and not uniformity in staff appointments, and to avoid cloning at senior staff level. A second incident which gave me a salutary lesson was my refusal one day to discuss some contentious issue any further with a head of department. Later that day I came across a quotation: 'All silencing of discussion is an assumption of infallibility' (John Stuart Mill). The next day I went to see the head of department in his office, and we managed to settle the issue that was drawing us apart. It was interesting to realise that different colleagues responded to different styles of leadership – those who were loaded with problems would more readily accept an arbitrary decision from myself to save them further mental turmoil, whilst those who were coping well always responded to democratic debate. Often when heads of department and I were engaged in discussion, the most productive ideas emerged when I agreed to sit back and merely listen to colleagues for half an hour in an attempt to free them from my own prejudice. It was all a matter of finding the right approach to get the best out of individuals, and it was a constant learning process.

With the 1970s approaching, and further education expanding rapidly, we had already put in our bid for a building extension based upon careful extrapolations of full-time student numbers and a growing demand for adult courses. This in turn made me realise that the college was quickly getting to the point where it was essential for me to have a deputy, and I presented my arguments to the Chief Education Officer, reluctantly accepting that it would take much time for a decision to be reached because of the need to refer the proposal to a whole series of Education Authority committees. Looking ahead again, there was the prospect of having to establish a statutory representative body of staff and students, to be known as the Academic Board, which was intended to have a great influence on the delivery of academic provision and the running of the college. I could already anticipate that this might create more problems than it would solve and might lead particularly to increased bureaucratic procedures in what had hitherto been routine matters. One or two older Principals with whom I discussed this proposal, which was already being actively discussed within the Department of Education and Science, were appalled at the prospect of losing much of their power and becoming bogged down in tedious discussion of mundane matters.

There were two other developments that lay ahead at this time. The first of these was the prospect of local government re-organisation as a result of the Redcliffe-Maud report of 1969. Although that report was not to be implemented, other schemes for boundary revisions were adopted, as a result of which our college was to come within a new county and therefore under the control of another Local Education Authority. Unfortunately it was an authority about whom many of us, who professed to know about these matters, had misgivings because of its smaller assets. Secondly, I was convinced that within the next decade all post-16 education would be based on single institutions, in theory for ideological reasons, since this could be seen as the corollary to the comprehensive school, which was now coming into vogue, and in practice because it might be more economical to have mega-institutions, rather like supermarkets. I was not

159

sure in my own mind whether I would relish the prospect of fighting to turn the college into one of these larger institutions or whether, to the contrary, there might be no such prospect at all under the new authority.

It was not easy to foresee how things would develop, but amongst those with a more informed view were the HM Inspectors who watched college affairs with interest. I had no idea at the time just how much they really did know about what was going on regionally and nationally in further and higher education, but whether you consulted with the General Inspector or the Specialist Subject Inspectors you could always be sure to get information and sound advice. They also always seemed to be on good terms with the Local Education Authority, with whom they conferred frequently on such matters as building programmes and educational policy. Those of us who, like myself, had the opportunity to meet them regularly realised that they were all talented professionals engaged in a very wide network of educational channels. Looking back, I remembered that HMI had given me beneficial advice at significant stages throughout my career, and so it was hardly surprising that I sometimes wondered if I could do the HMI's job, although I did not presume to put the idea directly to any that I already knew. Then, when an advertisement appeared in the educational press inviting applicants for HMI posts in a variety of specialisms, including General Studies, I decided to try my luck. It was at that point that I divulged my intention to my own employees and received their support. During the same week I had an angry letter from a local head teacher who had at last given way to my insistence that our enrolment of one of his sixth formers WAS in order in accordance with rule number something or other of the education committee's guidance regulations in this matter. He said, and I thought this might be an omen: 'With a mentality like that you would make a good senior government official.'

Ten weeks later I was rigorously interviewed at the Department's headquarters in Curzon Street, London, by a small group of senior members of the Inspectorate. Despite their courtesy and charm, I knew I was in for a real examination, with a startling economy of words to begin with: 'The obvious question – what's your answer to it?' Why indeed did I want to give up my 'present position and power'? Once this was disposed of, there followed an in-depth series of questions about my present post. How do you establish good relations with your heads of department? How do you know whether your teachers are any good? How do you see the essential relationship between HM Inspectors and the college Principal? How do you achieve consultation with a college? How do you feel about the prospect of Academic Boards? All this was followed by other, more specific, questions about my earlier career. Later, I was asked what I saw as significant issues to be solved, and when I suggested Tertiary Education, this was not pursued. I was fortunate to have had the opportunity to speak frankly about my career and my own convictions. I felt certain by the end of the interview not only that I had really spoken my mind but that I had never before been so totally scrutinised. The conduct of the interview had been masterly and objective, but I had no idea whether I had satisfied their requirements.

Two weeks later I nervously opened the OHMS letter to find that I had been recommended for appointment as one of Her Majesty's Inspectors of Schools, this being the operative title despite the fact that my work would be in the post-school sectors of further, higher and adult education. However, I was not to get too excited just yet because the appointment was subject to the completion of 'further enquiries and other matters', nor was I to give in my notice until these enquiries were completed. Five weeks later, my appointment was confirmed, by which time someone had presumably checked to see that I had not been a member of any subversive political organisation and that I was medically fit. I was now able to tell friends and colleagues the good news, and I was cheered by the many letters I received. One fellow-Principal wrote to say that he envied me and

161

wished he did not have to be a Principal to earn a living wage, though he did not think he himself would make a good HMI. I had said to him that I was not deluding myself into thinking the new role would be any more free from difficulties than my present one. To another fellow-Principal I wrote that 'whatever job we have in education, we are going to be faced by some mighty problems in the next decade.' So, despite the excitement I was aware I was not taking on an easy job. Yet there was one remark that stuck in my mind from a letter written by a retired HMI: 'Remember – the first year is the worst. After that, you're on your own for life.' It would be interesting to see if that proved to be true.

10

The Poacher Turned Gamekeeper

However distinguished the record of a candidate he will have to adjust himself to new conditions and do this at a relatively mature age... The sense of identity with a close-knit community may be lost for a time and so may the sense of authority with which an experienced teacher goes about his work... An inspector's work involves the need to travel at all seasons and to appear at his best with those for whom his visit is generally an infrequent event and often seen as an important one... The early months of his career can be both bewildering and stimulating.

HMI Today and Tomorrow, Department of Education and Science 1970

Only a minority of friends thought I was mad to have wanted an appointment as one of Her Majesty's Inspectors of Schools (HMI). Anyway, as those in the know explained, I was joining the ranks of the hundred or so whose job was to look at further and higher education establishments, not at schools. For the moment I was still overawed by the official notice, received three months before my starting date, telling me that THE QUEEN'S MOST EXCELLENT MAJESTY IN COUNCIL had been pleased to appoint myself and eight others as Her Majesty's Inspectors of Schools on the recommendation of the Secretary of State for Education and Science. I was to learn later that the first such orders of the Queen in Council had been made 130 years earlier.

As I began my appointment in September 1970 there were about 500 HM Inspectors in England, 47 in Wales, and a total teaching force in both countries of 400,000 for all schools and further education. It had not yet occurred to me to wonder how on earth so few inspectors could hope to assess so many teachers. For the moment I was very conscious of being the Queen's servant as I tried not too ostentatiously to display my newly acquired briefcase embossed with the royal crest. I had yet to work out in my mind whether I was the Man from the Ministry, guaranteed to receive an unctuous welcome on my future educational travels, or whether I should cultivate the image of special agent heading for trouble, though armed only with inspectorial files and a tiny Government security pass 'held subject to the provisions of the Official Secrets Act 1911–1939.' I felt quite excited when the production of this pass enabled me to penetrate into the appropriate Government building in the centre of Manchester.

Despite the courteous welcome from my fellow inspectors I soon realised that I had to know my place as a 'new boy'. I had to realise that I was, like all newly appointed HMI, on probation for the first year, and in that respect I was lucky because at one time the probationary period had been two years. It was rather like being an officer-cadet once again: you knew you were being watched and you had to be on your mettle. No matter what your previous experience, you were not going to be let loose for a long time. Even if you passed your probationary period with success, there would be much more to be learned after that. So for now, your initial training was in the hands of an experienced colleague who would act as your mentor and arrange for you to accompany various Inspector specialists on their travels. Their collective expertise covered a huge field of academic and vocational subject areas, from agriculture to textiles, together with general needs such as careers advice, counselling, education of the handicapped, multi-racial education, or teacher training, to name but a few. Each colleague that you accompanied would later be required to give your mentor a confidential comment on your professional performance.

It would all add up to visiting a great variety of institutions. You would be seeing things you had probably never seen before, whether a poor school in a socially deprived area or the inside of a top-security prison. You would often be away from home overnight, sometimes for several nights. Though you would concentrate on visits within your own regional area, you might also travel to other parts of the country for official meetings as well as inspections. You were expected to work excessive hours, and as soon as you returned to 'HQ' – your home – you would have to attend instantly to the flow of mail dropping through your letterbox – mostly brown envelopes emblazoned with the letters OHMS. As in all your previous professional experience, you would have to decide your priorities and to use your time economically. It would be essential, and even more so later on if you had made the grade, to keep careful records of everything and to meet deadlines when information was needed either by colleagues or by the 'Office' (the Department). As the quantities of papers on my desk began to increase, I began to think again of the advice given to me by one of the support staff in the Manchester office: 'Don't put too many papers together: they breed.'

I was lucky to have a sensitive and dedicated mentor, John, an experienced Inspector both of schools and colleges, and an expert in adult education. One of the first lessons I learned with him was to plan my journeys correctly and be ready for the unexpected. Once when I was en route to a rendezvous in Liverpool, I turned wrongly into a one-way road, but avoided the oncoming traffic in just enough time by escaping up a side road. Within moments I nearly repeated the same error as I continued my journey. Some months later I realised I was not alone in these travel problems, when I was a passenger in a small convoy of inspectors en route to a conference in Birmingham. We took a wrong exit three times in succession from the inner ring road and added about 30 unnecessary miles to our journey before safely reaching our destination. The fact is that there was much driving to be done, sometimes with fatal results. Two inspectors were killed during my early years of service. More often, there were summonses for speeding, and most of the offenders were women colleagues. Rumour had it that one Chief Inspector thought all new entrants to the Inspectorate should undergo a special driving test. I just kept hoping I would survive from day to day. Then a final lesson I learned from my mentor John was always to park my car ready for a quick getaway.

As I slowly began to cope more easily with crowded motorways and rush-hour traffic, I also became more used to the variable weekly agenda that came my way. Always there could be a sudden call to a completely different type of action, a metaphorical donning of one's 'bother boots' to accompany a colleague braving the enemy's fire. It seemed rather like that on the day I went with colleague Frank to a small local college, where according to the local authority's Director of Education there were some serious financial irregularities which he wanted us to investigate. We did not feel too happy as we arrived at the college, had a cautious conversation with the Principal, and then established that there was much overspending under the budgetary heading of part-time academic staff. We proceeded, as diplomatically as possible, to focus on one particular department and discovered that the number of tutorial groups in one of the courses had suddenly grown, as the head of department kept dividing the original class group into smaller and smaller units to give part-time employment to several unemployed friends. A month later, the head of department resigned, thus simplifying matters, but our visit did little to endear Her Majesty's Inspectors to the college academic staff. It led to our own in-house joke that 'we always go in pairs to . . .' This was in fact a rare exercise for HMI, and undertaken only to help a rather desperate Director of

166

Education whose worries led later to his own resignation through ill-health.

On another and happier occasion of a joint visit, I was returning from a primary school in the Cheshire countryside when my Inspector colleague Douglas stopped his car near to a farm. He had already demonstrated his knowledge of his own working patch by his clever choice of back roads to avoid the motorways. 'Now,' he said, 'I'm just going to buy some eggs, and while you're waiting, have a look on the other side of that hedge.' Without hesitation I pushed through the hedge where there was a slight gap. I was faced by a long low Nissen hut almost smothered on all sides by tall weeds and wild flowers. I foraged my way to the nearest window and peered into the empty building, which had once been the living quarters for airmen at this wartime camp. The main door was intact and the metal heating stove with its fat tin chimney was still in place. I remembered having to clean one of these during my own military service in a similar hut. 'Not many people know about this, oddly enough,' said Douglas on his return. 'The farmer never bothered to plough up this corner once he got the land back after the war. The runways have gone for good.' One or two cows were quietly lumbering in the vicinity. I looked around again, and we stood for a further moment in absolute silence. Other spirits were still there.

A few days later I accompanied another colleague, David, to a large penal institution, where we were due to inspect some of the adult education classes. As we were formally processed into the prison by a series of daunting personnel, I was already beginning to wish it was time to go home, but a more relaxed encounter with the Governor reassured us that we might expect early release. The more important business of seeing prisoners at work in the classroom proved enjoyable, for the tutors and students could well have been such as you would expect in any technical college. Convicted criminals look perfectly normal, as I quickly discovered, and they welcome an opportunity to get out of their prison cells and into the education block. There was such a pleasant and normal atmosphere that my colleague found himself saying to one prisoner, George, after an informal discussion about some novel the class was reading, 'Well, if you're here tonight I'll be able to resume this discussion.' It was a split second before we all laughed uproariously. He would certainly be there, though not necessarily in the education block.

As there was a long interval of time before some of the later classes, it was necessary for us to leave the institution for a few hours. When we returned, it was pitch black and pouring with rain. We stood outside the prison gate, having rung the doorbell for some time, and when challenged to state our business we had to roar several times in our loudest imperial tones, 'WE ARE HER MAJESTY'S INSPECTORS!' I imagined some bloody-minded prison officer deliberately taking his time. At last when we were eventually admitted, I was beginning to think it was harder to get into the prison than to get out of it. My colleague David in the course of our remaining visits to recreational classes did not in fact meet prisoner George again that night. David handed over copies of one or two useful pieces of literary criticism which the Education Officer promised to deliver. I was still thinking about one particular class we had visited, where in converted cell accommodation a crowd of other less literate prisoners was silently fashioning morose-looking teddy bears and other stuffed toys. It was still raining when we left the prison. The air was thoroughly damp, but welcome. That night I had troubled dreams.

I still had a long way to go in learning how to assess the teacher at work. Before fully acquiring that professional insight, I would be making many more days of visits with colleagues, as my probationary programme continued. At the same time, in parallel, there were opportunities to get an inside view of the organisation and particularly of my Further Education Inspector colleagues. One or two cynics outside the service would describe them as medieval robber barons, all competing in self-importance as they allegedly pushed to promote the power of the educational authorities to whom they gave official advice. Within our own ranks, our academic schools inspectors might regard them as of lower standing, the 'nuts and bolts' men, yet they included many highly qualified specialists, particularly in the sciences. My own impression was of a group of loyal, caring and committed individuals who fought hard to promote the virtues of technology, science, or business education. Just as the HMI assigned to inspect schools collectively monitored the progress of the statutory educational system, so the FE Inspectors were vital to the development of the further education system nationally.

I quickly learned during my probationary period that they were certainly respected in the colleges for the control they helped to exercise over major building programmes, even if some of their recommendations made to the Department could not please all applicants. Early on in my probationary year I attended one of our own committee meetings at which all the FE Inspectors had to decide how to advise the Secretary of State as to which applications for new technical college buildings, and extensions to existing colleges, should be approved. I witnessed an incisive yet fair-minded appraisal of technical education building priorities throughout the whole North-Western region, including the demolition of the case that I had made in my previous post for an extension to the college of which I had been Principal. It was an important lesson to come face to face with inspectors' individual and collective knowledge of further education establishments within their working region. Only with such knowledge could fair and economically sound recommendations be made.

This was another step in learning to take a broad view, first regional and then national, of the educational system. Since my work was to be mainly in the field of further and higher education, I waited with anticipation to attend my first annual conference of Further Education HMI at Cranfield. This was the gathering together of the force of about 100 colleagues, who between them somehow managed to monitor the progress and growth of post-school education throughout the land. Here were assembled not only those in the ranks but our most senior colleagues too. One of the first procedural activities in our plenary assembly was for the 'new boys' to stand up and be counted, and it was interesting to spot, perhaps for the first time, those other probationers who were being put through the mill, as each of us tried to smile with modest charm. Our most senior colleagues varied enormously in their attitudes, some conscious of their rank, others only too pleased to put you at your ease. The conference agenda was quickly worked through, with encouraging noises from one or two visiting permanent officials who welcomed the opportunity to escape from the confines of their London headquarters in order, as it were, to talk to the troops. Within the ordinary ranks, there was pleasant comradeship and the opportunity to conclude a number of useful arrangements for our future working programmes.

Over the rest of my probationary year I was at last beginning to appreciate the full scope of the HMI's work, which was seldom realised outside the service. The average college lecturer would see little of the individual HMI, imagining he or she just dropped into college on a whim. In reality HMI would never visit any college without prior notification, and it could be for different purposes. First, HMI might visit as a subject specialist – to see the teaching of, for example, Physics or Business Studies, concentrating on the work in a specific department of the college. Secondly, HMI might come, like a visiting uncle, as the assigned General Inspector in order to find out how the college is getting on in all its affairs. Conversation with the Principal might reveal problems with the local education authority. Ideas gathered in the college would reflect the general health, or otherwise, of the college. Thirdly, HMI in the role of District Inspector would liaise with the Chief Education Officer of the authority. Through these various roles the inspectors would be using their own reporting procedures to advise the Government of the day on the exact state of the education system nationally. They would therefore in the course of their work both exercise an advisory function and also contribute, it was hoped, to the improvement of the work they inspected.

What this meant in practice was that inspectors were always on the move and on the alert, as their assignments to inspect were not just restricted to one college. As subject specialists, they would be required to visit all the further education establishments in their region, probably as many as 30 or 40. As District Inspectors they would be assigned to give advice to one or two local education authorities. They would then keep in touch with each authority's problems as well as its progress, and usually they would be acting as the General Inspectors of its individual colleges. When they were not busy travelling around to colleges or municipal town halls, they would be attending in-house meetings arising from their own work or, from time to time, external meetings of educational bodies who sought their advice as well. Then, when they were not engaged at their office desks trying to write their various reports, they might be anxiously collating an appropriate request for comment to the Secretary of State, who was due to be asked a very difficult Parliamentary Question within 48 hours, or some-times less. In between times, they might well be planning the next specialist teachers' short course as part of the Department of Education's annual programme of in-service education, or even trying to find a moment to write a paper on the teaching of their own specialist subject or on the latest crisis affecting further education provision. One's working day was often 12 hours; there were some vast distances to be travelled; many nights away from home; much less annual leave than teachers enjoy. In all, a full life.

Just before the end of my first year of service, I was required to submit a written report giving my own views of my probationary service. I had to leave it to others to judge whether I ask too many questions or worry too much about getting things right. So I was able to dwell on the positive aspects of my tutelage, such as the opportunity to see so much of education in so short a time, to witness the skills of colleagues at work, to become actively involved in inspection, and to learn continuously through analysing one's own experience. My eyes had been opened to the enormous number of constraints that affect educational provision, whether they are human, material, or organisational. I was still naive enough not to realise that the Inspectorate itself would be progressively affected in the years ahead by the effects of world events, political policies, rising unemployment and economic restraint. Apparently I said the right things, and as it seemed that I had not seriously blotted my copybook I was given fully fledged status a few weeks later, as were several other new recruits who had started their service with me but in other parts of the country.

In the immediate years ahead, I frequently met people outside the world of education who would ask me what I did for a living. The most telling encounters were usually during train journeys to London, where official business demanded our attendance. Initially with enthusiasm I would try to explain, only to be met with incomprehension. 'How can you be called an Inspector of Schools if you don't usually go to schools?' or 'How can you properly inspect things if you're so few in number?' or more irritatingly, 'Then which education authority do you work for?' Later, the cheap plastic briefcase, with its stamped royal crest denoting government service, became a less popular accoutrement. Many of us merged into anonymity by bearing only an orthodox sort of document case like any overworked businessman. It was standard procedure to withdraw into the privacy of our newspapers or working files, whichever happened to be of priority after the consumption of one of those gargantuan British Rail breakfasts that either kill or cure you for the rest of the day. Eventually I ceased to be surprised, on the occasions when someone did manage to embroil me in a conversation, that most people unconnected with education professionally have an incredibly naive view of what the educational system of this country really comprises or what education ought to be about. I also had many encounters with distraught fathers

172

anxious to ensure their sons or daughters fared better at school than they claimed to have done. I would often arrive home convinced that all is not well in the state of education. I would begin to wonder whether what I was doing for a living would have positive results.

If it was a pleasure to talk occasionally to someone who really wanted to know more about one's work or to be asked if the Secretary of State really was behind the latest headlined educational manoeuvre, it was never easy to explain one's work simply. Often it was helpful to say to a fellow-traveller, 'Imagine you're with me visiting a college. What are some of the first things we're going to notice?' Before long my listener would be working one or two things out for himself or herself and realising that HM Inspectors do not just drop in but come with a purpose, a friendly one, one hopes. Much depends, say in the case of a one-day visit, on whether it is the first of such visits, or a follow-up of a previous visit or even of a week's inspection by a team of specialists, or a visit being made specifically at the request of the Principal or a Head of Department, either or both of whom could be seeking your advice on a matter of policy, staff deployment, teaching techniques, or how to help newly appointed teachers. Often paradoxically it would be in colleges with the better reputation for standards that the most advice would be sought.

For a time, while Government policy did not prescribe the activities of Education Inspectors too closely, it was possible to allow oneself to be diverted into an unexpected and unplanned session with a whole group of teachers, at the expense of visiting all the classes one had hoped to see. Only an exceptionally cunning head of department would suggest an impromptu seminar to save colleagues from scrutiny in the classroom. It was always exceptional to find colleges being obstructive, however, and the necessity of writing up one's note of visit, which would be likely to be seen by other colleagues, obliged one to stick to one's original business.

'Well, what happens, then, if you're there for a whole

week of inspection?' was often the follow-up question If I was due to leave the train at the next station, I could duck that one. The brief answer was, 'It's rather a different ball-game.' I could throw the ball back to my listener and say, 'Suppose you're the Director of Education. Why do you want one of your colleges to be inspected? That's assuming the initiative came from your side. But supposing the Inspectors have suggested an inspection – what could that mean for good or for bad?' An inspection on a large scale might be to record good practice, so that others could be encouraged to follow the example set in, say, the use of buildings or the deployment of staff, or the delegation of responsibilities. On the other hand it might be instigated at the Director of Education's request in order to expose poor practice.

In one of the worst colleges I visited, the Principal had no idea of devolved responsibility and personally guarded major items of expensive teaching equipment in his own office, and seldom held a staff meeting except to give orders. His retirement, together with growing staff militancy, cleared the way for improvements, including the provision of an alternative in the college refectory to chips with everything. In the best colleges it would come as a surprise to many of the staff to be told at the end of an inspection that their work was very much above average. It was because Inspectors worked both regionally and nationally that they gained a true perception of standards throughout the whole educational system. Lecturers in colleges, on the other hand, worked largely in an isolated environment. Many of them welcomed an inspectorial evaluation, because it would put their work and their college in a broader context, both professionally and nationally. It would also lead to greater pressures, after an official inspection, to introduce better facilities both for staff and students.

It often happened, too, that colleges that had impressive policy statements failed to meet their own claims, and those that had either limited, or indeed no such statements of policy, were achieving very high standards. Certainly the

174

total scrutiny of a week's visit by a team of Inspectors would usually unearth the truth, even if it was modestly described in the Inspectors' own jargon as merely a 'snapshot'.

'But how does all this affect the teacher or lecturer under scrutiny?' was the next more discerning enquiry, assuming I had not left the train. Here we enter into the realms of sensitivity, for who really likes to be watched at work? Some people would say a lecturer or teacher is not going to behave normally if under observation. I well remember my own experiences of being assessed. The lecturer may feel this is the very last class he wanted to be inspected, and how much better it would have been if one of the more amenable groups of students could have been observed. Fortunately for me, the majority of lecturers that I visited when they were teaching Liberal Studies or English, responded to my own introductory comment that I was there to share their approach and to learn from it. The most difficult experience was always where there had been no previous contact with an Inspector, so that the lecturer's fear or suspicion of being branded a failure had to be dispelled. Sometimes I found that it was helpful to let the students ask me questions as to why I was there, which would give me the opportunity to explain for a couple of minutes without seriously interrupting the proceedings that someone 'on high' – whether the Local Authority or the Government of the day – cared considerably about young people and their educational opportunities. Once the students were convinced I was not a hostile presence, they would respond well to the rest of the lesson. It was often a pleasing reflection on the loyalty of students to their lecturers that they rallied to support them with very mature behaviour.

Unfortunately it was not always easy to achieve a relaxed intrusion into a class, especially if, as happened during a prolonged period of inspection in a particularly large college on several different sites, you were having to visit as many as 30 or 40 classes during the week. Usually a preliminary meeting with members of staff prior to the inspection provided the chance to explain the problem from my own

175

point of view and at the same time in the more openly directed regimes to encourage lecturers to draw my attention to classes that they would particularly like me to visit. One group of students might be enacting a simulated crisis in the factory, illustrating the conflicting roles of foreman, site manager and other staff. Another group might be preparing a community enterprise that required consent from various authorities. In the course of time I found that it is possible to build up a fairly accurate picture of a department and a college from this kaleidoscope of class visits and incidental conversations with students and staff. Even in colleges that I thought I knew quite well, because I had been there before, the experience of a longer visit was always rewarding, not only in providing a revised view of everything but in creating opportunities to share information with staff and to encourage new approaches to old problems.

During this decade, the 1970s, further education colleges and technical colleges were undergoing many radical changes stemming from the economic situation and the general climate of thinking in our society, creating dilemmas and divisions that showed no signs of solution. At the college level courses were being re-shaped to reflect a greater awareness of the need to provide 'relevant' training that would arguably produce a better workforce and one more likely to increase this country's productivity and wealth. Every college visited was wrestling with the same primary problem – how to meet the demands of school leavers. The gradually worsening employment situation meant that students were choosing to continue their education rather than risk failing to find work. In the past, colleges had catered for two distinct groups, those who wanted a more or less academic course with a view to going on to higher education, and those who wanted vocational training of a specific kind, leading to employment. Now, gradually, colleges were becoming packed with youngsters who did not want necessarily job-specific courses, nor courses that were heavily academic, and this was leading to newly devised curricula emerging at national level and newly devised approaches to learning, particularly as Information Technology was making its impact. As each year went by, I encountered more and more gloom in the colleges, stemming from the confusion of new curricular demands on teachers for whom, because of limited financial resources, it was not possible to provide new training and staff development. It was not unknown for technical college lecturers to seek early retirement or other employment to escape the growing pressures.

I noticed also that students were becoming much more reflective about their own experiences of education and training. In one city college, whilst visiting a lively class of young school leavers on a GCE course which might later on lead to a career in nursing, I was given a piece of writing that touched upon the root of many problems. Sarah, aged 17, explained: 'I am attending college because I don't want to get a job. It is difficult to know what I would like to gain from college besides more qualifications. Really I would like to go to university, though I don't know what I want to do.' Sarah claimed to have hated school and offered an unusual confession: 'I never skived but for all I did in lessons e.g. read magazines at the back of the class and laugh, I might as well have stayed at home. No, that's not exactly true, because while I was reading I had to keep one eye and ear open for the teacher. This taught me awareness, and I also discovered I had the ability to do two things at once. I actually absorbed more information like this than if I were sitting there day-dreaming.' She went on to explain that some of her friends who copied her example did badly in their exams, while she confounded her teachers by coming out near the top. Nevertheless she had been castigated in school reports as lazy, and was now hoping to thrive within a different educational regime.

I expected that Sarah would indeed thrive in this college, which was considered by myself and colleagues to be one of the best of its kind, with competent staff, well-behaved students, a pleasant environment, and a supportive Edu-

177

cation Authority. Yet I was intrigued to find out that the college had a serious problem because of one out of every seven students withdrawing prematurely from their courses, in all four departments. The withdrawal rate had almost doubled in the academic years 1976 to 1978. A specially commissioned investigation at the behest of the college Governors established that there was no one predominant cause but a variety of key factors – such as leaving to take up employment when an opportunity occurred, or emotional, domestic, or financial considerations, or even the simple fact that the student could not cope with the academic level of study. Other colleges throughout the country were having similar problems, giving weight to the case for the growth of more generalised introductory courses for school leavers, many of whom were beginning to feel members of a 'no hope society'. All this also underlined the need for colleges to have student counsellors capable of giving expert advice on employment and personal problems, yet because of financial stringency such appointments were not always made.

In the meantime, much of my time was still being spent in looking at the teaching of those elements of courses described as General or Liberal Studies. These subjects, much as they had been when I had taught them earlier in my career, were still recognised as something in contrast to students' main technical or business studies, and designed to help them as young people, not as future earners. Often, even where such General or Liberal Studies were imaginatively devised and well delivered by lecturers, there were technical studies lecturers who resented the time 'stolen' from the overall timetable, and the students themselves shared this prejudice. Some students, again as I knew well from my own teaching experience, would not hesitate to declare these General Studies as 'boring', or to manifest their indifference through revealing body language or the simple technique of shrinking physically behind a strategically erected mound of crash helmets and leather jackets. It was not always easy, as a visiting Inspector, to offer suitable advice.

As a member of a team of specialist Inspectors who assessed these courses throughout the country, my job within my own working region was to encourage good practice and to make lecturers aware of new approaches being demanded by the Government, or by employers, or by the college themselves in response to the changing employment situation. Unfortunately, it was always the bad lessons that caught the headlines, giving rise to the belief that most General Studies lecturers were long-haired left-wing subversives with degrees in Sociology and drug-taking, and prepared to talk about anything salacious to keep the apprentices quiet for an hour. Such a notion did an injustice to those faithful zealots who genuinely set out to make their student apprentices more literate and numerate. There was even full support in some colleges from the technical staff who carried the major teaching load of technology and specialised skills. Both they and the General Studies lecturers would respond with interest to new curricular ideas. So it was usually the more run-of-the-mill General Studies lecturers who openly resented the newer trends in further education, as was confirmed by my experience of running a one-day course for local college lecturers. I had spent the best part of the day giving a careful introduction to the idea of considering a more objective approach to one's teaching, stressing the value of defining more precisely what one hoped to achieve in a lesson, and suggesting ways for the lecturer to assess his own performance. In the final session, one of the lecturers whom I had persuaded to attend this one-day course, stood up and said, 'I think this day has been a complete waste of time.' Fortunately, others disagreed. For me, it was back to the drawing board later to anticipate the next move, including how to talk to him when I made my next visit to his college.

Our own morale as Inspectors was not yet too depressed by events, for the onset of new ideas and new course provision became a challenge. If you believed, as we did, that much needed to be done to improve standards and therefore to create better opportunities for students, you were willing to contribute, as we all did, to the drafting of an all-embracing educational document that would spell out the new wisdom. I found myself saying year after year, when I was visiting colleges, 'Well, you'll find things clearly explained in the new pamphlet, when it appears.' The word of Inspectors was still respected and still awaited during those years. Everybody kept on waiting. Unfortunately, the pamphlet was never published, allegedly a victim of the internal conflicting politics of the Department and the Inspectorate, and allegedly blue-pencilled by Mrs Margaret Thatcher as Secretary of State in the early 1970s, on the grounds that it was too left-wing and too ambitious in its objectives. However, there were many colleges that continued to resist the philosophy that nothing should be taught unless it can be seen to be vocationally useful. Many full-time students continued to have opportunities for some form of recreational and cultural activities, including music, art, drama, or debate on current issues. In the more enterprising colleges, students successfully took an active part in community projects intended to broaden their horizons.

The same sort of concern in this period was affecting sixth forms and the emerging sixth-form colleges, especially after the raising of the school-leaving age to 16 in 1973. In my visits to look at general studies amongst sixth formers, I found this similar conflict between the utilitarian demands for good A-level results and the recognition that subjects ought to be taught in such a way as to develop the whole person. Only the exceptional teacher could achieve both these ends through the actual academic teaching, but students definitely profited from the more adult atmosphere, and often the more generous resourcing, of such colleges. My work also gave me the opportunity to compare the development of another large group of youngsters, those in employment who, whilst not apprentices, were sent to a college once a week to study for a professional qualification.

Here again, students themselves were concentrating narrowly on getting through an exam. They would have little incentive to become interested in anything else the college might have to offer, and little time or opportunity to mix with other course students. In one enquiry I initiated, starting from the premise that as the Government was encouraging greater day release, its own departments would be enthusiastic promoters, I found students from three government departments had fewer chances of day release than those in commercial employment, simply because the growing workload made it impossible to lose young staff from the workplace for one day per week. In any case, older established staff who had not been given day release in the past often resented their younger colleagues having such opportunities.

Problems and unrest seemed to be springing from an ever-growing variety of sources. One of the most traumatic innovations was the onset of training courses promoted by the Manpower Services Commission, to which the colleges began to respond in line with Government policy. I can still remember the concern felt by my own colleagues, who feared that their own work was to be undermined by the arrival of a new army of bureaucrats who knew little about education, even if they knew slightly more about training. I was frequently surprised, sometimes appalled, to discover what inadequate accommodation had been put into use for certain youth opportunity or vocational preparation courses in colleges that were already overcrowded but under pressure to respond to government training initiatives. Often, too, such training courses were being staffed by the least experienced college lecturers, though many of them at least believed in the validity of helping the young unemployed. I sometimes found it difficult to report objectively on such courses when I felt they were mainly a means of reducing the unemployment statistics for the age groups between 16 and 18. Many of my colleagues shared my sense of gloom, which was further deepened by a 1978 management review of the Department of Education and Science that failed to address the absurdity of having an inspectorate now of only 400 Inspectors, who by diverse means were expected to monitor the whole of the educational system with more than half a million teachers and more than 30,000 establishments – and to give quick evaluations of every new educational development.

I can imagine my talkative and inquisitive fellow traveller on the Inter-City train saying, 'Well, I'm still not clear how you assess the teachers that you see. What are you looking for? What do you expect?' I'm prompted to reply, 'I sometimes wonder. I've done it so many times that it's just automatic, like joyless sex. But when I'm feeling more active and responsive, I'm alert to everything. You look immediately at the lecturer and the students. You listen to the tone of voice. You observe the body language. You feel the atmosphere, physical, emotional, intellectual. You begin to tune in. You notice the style of teaching and learning. Is it appropriate to what the lecturer's trying to achieve? How are the students responding? Taking notes? Asking questions? Not being allowed to ask questions? Is there a content of information that's being put across? If so, is the method appropriate? Does the lecturer vary the activities throughout the lesson, finding an acceptable mix of, say, listening, talking, reading, writing, looking, thinking, doing, and so on? Can you see if the lecturer is aiming to impart knowledge, affect attitudes, or develop specific skills whether manual or intellectual? No checklist can give you the complete guide, however. In the end, you're guided by the overall impression. Interestingly, when you've been looking at a great number of classes, anything from twenty or more during an extended inspection, and you come to write it up possibly a day or two later, or even a week later if you've been off on another ploy, you find your mind has distilled the whole experience and you manage to express the essence in only a few hundred words instead of thousands. Well, usually that is.

I'll tell you more if we meet again . . .'

182

11

Watching the Estate

Watch ye, stand fast in the faith . . . be strong.
Let all your things be done with charity.

I Corinthians 16.13

I eventually set out to have a chat with the lecturer who had
slammed the 'new approach' at the recent day conference.
On the day of my visit to his college I failed to locate him,
but over a cup of tea in the refectory one of his colleagues
summed things up: 'No money, no equipment, no promotion
in this bloody department.' Like his critical colleague, he
found his life frustrating, but he really cared about his
students. I tried to let him see that I shared his concern to
help young people. He seemed too bitter to notice. Then it
was time for me to move on to the next task. That was
always the problem – never enough time.

There was always much more to my job than just assessing
the lecturer's performance. Sometimes I felt like an ill-
prepared coach recommending body-building exercises to
an under-nourished client who had no prospect of getting a
better diet. At other times my morale was restored when I
met lecturers who loved the challenge of new ideas and
could always use them to advantage. During any working
week I might experience both extremes, and over the
passage of years see a remarkable range of provision. What
I had always loosely thought of as the education system
after school was in fact a myriad of providing systems, trying

to respond to the turmoil of events in the 1970s and 1980s, especially the continuing problem of creating appropriate courses for youngsters whose job prospects were seriously declining. I found myself more and more concerned for young people and their lack of prospects, no matter what their levels of ability. It was hard at times to conceal one's own private feelings during visits to colleges, or to avoid getting into open arguments about Government policy. A very patient older colleague facetiously used to tell me to turn to the New Testament and recall St Paul's advice to the Corinthians. We should learn to be 'Giving no offence in anything, that the ministry be not blamed' and showing 'much patience in afflictions, in necessities, in distresses.'

After my brief visits to penal institutions during the early years of my service, I was privately thankful when no major assignments of this kind came my way. Then suddenly duty called again, and I was unexpectedly assigned to assist in the full inspection of the educational provision in two high-security prisons. On each occasion I joined with my colleagues early in the morning outside the prison gates and became absorbed into the daily queue of permanent staff waiting to get into the prison. Once inside, my colleagues and I were escorted throughout the different areas of the prison, with constant unlocking and relocking of doors. Perversely, I found myself watching and noting, as if I was a genuine prisoner being taken to confinement. The next moment I would be looking out for an attack party poised to overpower the guard or take us all hostage. I tried to dismiss such absurd thoughts. There was no threat to your personal safety, but you still felt you had to move quietly and without pomp, until you finally reached the safe haven of the education wing. You had already been carefully observed by successive prison officers, the most forbidding being the 'Chief', who usually had the charisma of a time-serving Regimental Sergeant Major. Nothing or nobody proceeded without his approval.

As I moved along, I suddenly remembered the story told to me by a colleague, Robert, about his visit to another prison. Apparently, shortly after Robert was admitted, one of the prison officers was certain that Robert was an imposter. Robert was quickly confronted. 'May I see your ID (identity card)?' was a request that he could not meet, because it was not the policy of our own government department to issue us with IDs. Usually this did not cause any problems, but on this occasion there was a huge problem, because Robert had never known until then that he looked like a much-wanted Irish terrorist. With relief on all sides, the crisis was quickly overcome. As for myself, I was thankful not to receive any such special scrutiny.

Inside the education wing, there was a semblance of normality. The teaching staff, a mixture of full-time and part-time lecturers provided by the Local Education Authority, worked hard. Their teaching ranged from adult literacy to Open University classes. Some of the teachers were amongst the most dedicated I have ever met. They never felt any personal risk, because they knew that the inmates who came to classes were glad to escape from their cells into a more civilised atmosphere and wanted to keep this privilege. These teachers knew too that there were certain people who resented the idea of convicted prisoners being given such opportunities to better themselves. It was common knowledge that some of the prison officers shared this view, so when there were official ongoing staff disputes over pay, or deployment of personnel, the escorting of prisoners to classes was cancelled, and the education pro-gramme was put on hold.

If you are privileged, as I felt I was, to sit in with a class of lifers studying a literary text, you notice the evident pleasure each student gets from escaping into another world and being able to talk without inhibition about the charac-ters, feelings and incidents depicted in, say, a novel. Each class member is establishing a bond with the author, and understanding for example what Thomas Hardy meant when he said: 'My novels are the result of long thoughts about familiar things.' Then suddenly, as the visiting Inspec-tor, you realise there are constraints. The class may be

185

discussing a character or an action in the text, but the inmates carefully have to avoid any talk about their sentences and the acts that led to them, for that is the accepted convention. Not to have such a constraint could lead to great difficulties for the tutor. Knowing this as a visitor, you admire the skill of the tutor who treads carefully, establishes an easy relationship with the class members, and succeeds in making this a perfectly normal sort of educational process. Yet still you suddenly find yourself rather like a voyeur, silently wondering, 'Which one stabbed his wife?' or 'Who was the one that murdered his father?' Just as quickly you dismiss these wild thoughts. You remind yourself that most capital crimes are committed in the heat of the moment by perfectly ordinary people. You complete your temporary mental aberration by recalling your own past moments of madness ... and you say to yourself, 'There but for the grace of God go I.' Once again you concentrate on the lesson in progress. You realise that for most of the class members this is more than an escape from the prison cell. It is still a real piece of education for all of them – and for myself.

My own role and that of my colleagues during these visits was simply to look at education provision, not at the whole prison. Usually my time was spent visiting small classes held either in the education wing or occasionally in alternative teaching space formed by knocking two cells into one. The task of fully evaluating the overall working of any penal establishment was undertaken by the Prison Department's own Inspectorate. Though it was not for myself and colleagues to be asking questions beyond matters of educational provision, I could not help but wonder about the whole system of incarceration and the inevitable stresses and strains that are part of it. On one occasion, outside working hours, I happened to meet a prison officer who had needed six months to recover from injuries received during an altercation with one or two inmates. The other side of the picture, as given in the many published accounts of former prisoners, can be just as distressing. Having read a number of these, and having also reflected on my admittedly short visits to more than 12 penal establishments, I certainly believe that life within the prison walls has never been easy for prisoner, or for permanent staff, or for the teachers who commit themselves to providing an education service.

My brief but official contacts with Prison Governors opened my eyes a little further. One Monday morning I was ushered by appointment into the inner sanctum of a large top-security prison as an introductory courtesy procedure. The Governor quickly explained that his immediate problem was sorting out an incident that had occurred at 5.30 a.m. that very day – a prisoner had set fire to his mattress and died as a result of asphyxiation. Already the necessary investigation was under way. I felt it was remarkable that the Governor still found time to talk to me when he could easily have handed me over to one of his Assistant Governors, though they were probably busy with the investigation. Even this brief conversation was enough to reveal his deep sense of compassion and his calmness in a crisis. A much more homely meeting had occurred earlier in my service when the Governor of a large open prison, with a much more relaxed and materially productive regime, presented me with some of the prison's home-grown fruit and vegetables. Neither of us felt involved in any act of corruption. This Governor was a caring man, whose example inspired hope within the more relaxed regime of his establishment.

On the whole I always felt relieved to get back to my more traditional duties of inspecting in colleges, though I had learned over the years that new assignments would often crop up at any time. It so happened that in 1978 I was required to join the ranks of our inspectors who were invited by the Ministry of Defence to observe the training of junior soldiers, junior leaders, and Army apprentices. The inspection of junior soldier regiments and Army apprentice colleges had a long history. I followed a succession of Inspectors, all with war service, who inspected the educational element in the overall programme of training given to all these youngsters who had volunteered at the age of 16. They would later be able to start full adult service, usually at about the age of 18. At different times over a number of years I was a visitor to most of the Army's junior units in different parts of the country, accompanied by appropriate inspector colleagues. On most occasions I was assigned as the 'Reporting Inspector', which meant planning the exercises in conjunction with the Director of Army Education's staff. All this gave me the opportunity to see just how effectively the Army could motivate young school leavers, many of whom had not prospered at school. With this added training behind them, the former juniors were usually well in the lead when they started as adult soldiers. Some would eventually achieve commissioned rank.

It would be easy, but mistaken, for people brought up on a diet of early 'Carry On' films, or recalling National Service or even war service, to imagine that the Army would be an insentive, bureaucratic organisation hardly equipped to deal with young adolescents other than to impose strict discipline and to order 'short back and sides'. I have to admit that in one of my early official visits the length of my own hair did seem to cause a few eyebrows to be lifted. I remembered for subsequent visits to be less tonsorially offensive to my Army hosts, to have an immaculate crease in my trousers, and to give my shoes a proper polish. This was merely a matter of courtesy. What was much more important was to discover the pride that the units took in achieving standards in all respects that would match those of any civilian establishment, especially in the teaching of the fundamental skills of communication. It was a delight to see the way that these youngsters would quickly develop confidence in addressing a group in order to give a briefing or to issue orders. In the same way they would develop team spirit as well as the ability to think quickly in a crisis situation. These were qualities developed both in the class-room and on the training fields, thanks to the combined skills and team work of the RAEC (Royal Army Educational Corps), the civilian lecturers, and the permanent military staff.

Those officers and NCOs that we met always welcomed the chance to enter into discussion. In one infantry unit I remember the training officer who, when asked what he thought was the primary objective in the junior soldiers' programme, replied, 'To put fire in their bellies!' This led later to many a prolonged discussion sometimes with Army personnel, sometimes within our own ranks, over the whole range of intentions for these youngsters at this stage. If you accept that the infantryman of the future must know how to respond instantly and accurately with his rifle fire, you can recognise the need for rigorous and repetitive training to condition that response. Nearly two decades after the time I am describing, there was an outcry over the case of the soldier in Northern Ireland who fired too many shots at what was taken to be a hostile vehicle. There would have been no such problem in a real battlefield situation. Military trainers today have the delicate job of teaching trainees to observe some difficult constraints, especially in what is often hypocritically regarded as a peace situation. As I saw for myself, this sort of problem had to be confronted in the training of all Army juniors, particularly those who were later likely to operate in the field, on patrol, or on sentry duty in any troubled area of the world. Long after the inspections had ceased, many of my colleagues when we met again would remember the need for 'fire in our bellies', but we were thankful we were not likely to be issued with rifles and put in really life-threatening situations. A few verbal blasts from unhappy lecturers were preferable to live bullets.

My respect for the Army's achievement with young entrants from school rapidly increased during the period of my assignments. What particularly impressed us was the care that was taken to monitor the welfare of all the junior entrants. First of all, in the company lines all officers and NCOs were specially selected for their experience in handling youngsters. Some in fact had started their careers as junior soldiers. The system had been nurtured to ensure little likelihood of brutality or abuse, and even in the most demanding training situations all the young soldiers were scrupulously watched, despite the intense rigour that could occur with, say, obstacle courses or gruelling field exercises. Any of the youngsters who could not make the grade had the opportunity to give up their service, but not many did. There were other networks deliberately developed to provide the necessary safety valves in the form of persons to whom someone in distress could turn. Army Chaplains of different religious denominations or civilian staff, such as the WRVS lady (affectionately known in some units as the 'Regimental Mum') – all played an important part by being available for a private chat. Homesickness, anxiety about domestic matters, and most personal problems could be capably but sympathetically dealt with. Really critical problems led to quick contact with parents, who in any case received periodic written reports from the unit. In one Army college, a typical apprentice said to me, 'It did great things for your morale to be able to talk to Majors and Colonels as if they were your own friends, not forgetting the tremendous sense of humour of the senior NCOs.' It was not really surprising that when parents were invited to Open Days to see the units, they could hardly believe what high standards their sons had achieved. Somehow the Army was turning ordinary school leavers, many of whom had languished in the lower streams of secondary education, into young persons with demonstrable self-discipline and self-reliance. Many of them had also successfully been involved in the unit's community enterprises, raising money for the disabled, putting on gymnastic displays, or giving a band performance, often competing nationally.

Our own participation as visiting Inspectors was always subject to our other commitments in the public sector of education. The Army was also constantly reviewing its own commitments. Hence there had to be a great deal of discussion to decide not only which units were to be inspected, but which Inspectors could be made available to make up the necessary team of specialists. My own task as Reporting Inspector was to liaise with the Army before the inspection, agree the programme, head the team of Inspectors, and later write the official report incorporating all the written comments of my colleagues. It was an unwritten convention that an early draft of the report would be seen on the Army side, enabling us to amend any factual inaccuracies and if necessary to modify any observations that might stir up a hornet's nest. Following each inspection and usually with a senior colleague, I had to make a visit to the Ministry of Defence in London to report personally to the Major-General in charge of Army Education. For the former lad with thin legs, the infant playing at soldier, who had marched to the tunes of Sousa, or even for the erstwhile young subaltern of the Royal Engineers, this should have been an awesome experience. It was the first time, but not subsequently. As ever, I realised that people who achieve high rank frequently do so because of their capacity to behave without pomposity. They also know how to use their time economically, and they expect others to do the same. On the occasions when it was made clear to me that our debriefing session should last no more than an hour, I always felt pleased to have finished my own oral report within a minute of the time allocated to me.

It was interesting, too, to realise that the Ministry of Defence was, like other Government departments, being subjected to severe financial cuts. The whole provision of Army junior establishments was therefore under threat, and with this knowledge our reports sometimes muted our criticism where we had observed insufficient educational equipment or too few opportunities for the in-service training of education staff. We might say 'as and when circumstances permit, it is recommended that further thought should be given to the acquisition of . . .' This really meant 'we well understand there's no money for . . . and all of us know you'll be lucky if things ever improve.' On the whole, I realised that Army education personnel were better able

191

to grit their teeth in the face of expenditure cuts than many of their civilian counterparts in the public sector. They were too wise and well-disciplined to air their complaints in public. They were also philosophical enough, after 1982, to see that without the financial priorities decided by the Ministry of Defence, often resulting in less money for Army junior units, the Falklands War might have been a disaster.

All this was not only another interesting slice of my inspectorial career but an education in itself. However, the rest of my duties continued with frequent visits to colleges, and meetings both with colleagues and with outside concerns such as training boards, or with Local Education officers. Then, as if to prove my point about new assignments being always on the way, I began to become involved in the provision of a series of national courses to be attended by administrators, heads and teachers from a representative sample of schools and colleges. The purpose was to reflect upon educational provision for the 14-to-19 age group, which was becoming an ever-increasing matter of concern to the government of the day. By a drastic coincidence one of these courses, or really minor conferences, opened a few days after the riots in Toxteth, Liverpool in July 1989. A more appropriate prelude could not have been imagined, let alone engineered, to illuminate the need for education and training for the 14-to-19 age group. Our opening speaker, the Most Reverend Derek Warlock, the Archbishop of Liverpool, came to us immediately after a meeting with the Prime Minister, Mrs Margaret Thatcher, who had made a special visit to the city. Not often does a speaker at such a course have such a demanding preliminary assignment, nor have to face a journey through baying crowds. The Archbishop, in the calmer atmosphere of the educational assembly, quickly reminded us of the tremendous challenge to be faced in providing education for younger people who live in an area of social deprivation and unemployment, where the existence of a multi-racial society creates further needs. We were left with no doubts about

192

the immense challenge of working for reconciliation, not confrontation.

Later that week course members heard a headmaster deliver a first-hand account of a riot in an inner-city school, reflecting unresolved issues that will continue to challenge our complacency for ever. This headmaster had worked hard for 11 years to establish his secondary school as a community facility. Situated amidst debilitated housing areas, with vandalised high-rise buildings, the school had been opened to the whole populace for 50 weeks in the year, seven days a week, offering social and educational sustenance on top of its schooling for the children. This was an area of closely knit families and streets, of empty shops, of mass unemployment. It was a fact of life that nearly half the children in school were 'at risk', according to the Social Services department. Some of the girls aged 12 to 16 were working as clubland prostitutes, to create family income. Boys too were earning money, through homosexual activity. As for conventional job opportunities, these had vanished. Yet the head and his staff soldiered on in the belief that education must have something to offer. The school buildings were not well maintained by the local authority because of lack of money, but they were obviously respected by all their users, unlike some of the housing estates. In its first year, the school had attracted 24,000 people into the premises, reaching out into the community, trying to offer the opportunity for life-long education. Nearly every part of the school continued to be available for the community to use.

The build-up to inner-city riots during this period produced its own sudden eruption in this particular school, in hideous contradiction of all the good things being attempted. First of all, about 40 children refused to go into school one day when required. One of them came to the fore and addressed the group with a Fascist-style tirade that he could not possibly have composed by himself. The staff managed to keep the school under some semblance of control. The next day, 150 pupils walked out from lessons,

193

intimidating other pupils who would not join them. A few pupil demonstrators were spitting at a coloured teacher. Before long, windows were being broken, and certain members of staff were being stoned. Curious complaints were being shouted – about the school timetable, or about school rules. The next day, similar events occurred. Finally, after an extraordinary period of restrained response by the staff, the police were called in to restore order. They discovered that some of the pupils agitating were not even members of that school. Other strangers had been handing out leaflets calling for rebellion against 'petty rules and bad conditions'. A carefully orchestrated 'rebellion' had been performed, relying on fear, prejudice, gullibility and adolescent bravado.

Several views emerged from this traumatic upheaval, as explained to a number of course members who subsequently were able by arrangement to visit the school. Possibly many of the youngsters had been influenced by seeing riotous behaviour in television news reports. Some, in fact, had taken part in the main riots in the city. Others naively took part in the school disturbance from a sense of mischief. These same pupils, talking courteously to their visitors, claimed to like their school, and said on the whole they accepted school discipline. They supported the school's programme of extra-curricular activities, and they were seen to be relating well to the many adults who also used the school. Other independent enquiries had indicated that the headmaster and staff had behaved with exemplary patience throughout the period of upheaval. Finally, it was recorded that the parents officially consulted after the event were genuinely horrified by what had happened. The headmaster summed it all up with these words: 'It could happen to any one of you. It's a terrible experience.'

During the early 1980s, through this and other subsequent courses, I met many representatives from schools and colleges who felt a similar sense of anguish. These were not the academic trendies so often depicted in the popular press as being responsible for all the ills of society. These were men and women of integrity, perplexed as teachers, bewildered as parents, anxious to understand the young, and keen to be effective educators in the face of a rapidly changing society beset with so many apparent ills. Our job as the Inspectors organising the courses was to put them in a think-tank for a week. No-one escaped a confrontation with micro-technology – chips with everything. No-one was allowed to ignore the fact that micro-technology is widening the gap between those who get jobs and those who do not. 'Work' itself was needing another definition, to take account of the fallacy that its only form is paid employment. It was one thing to wonder how you might spend your time if you were suddenly relieved, as in winning the pools, of the need to make money, and another completely different scenario to imagine yourself as a school-leaver who might never have a job. Clearly there was no easy answer to finding the right paths in education and training for youngsters. In the meantime, unemployment amongst the 16-to-24 age group was two to three times higher than in any other age group. No wonder the Government was anxious not just to preserve its own life but to press the schools and colleges into finding a new way forward.

Many of the course members, feeling those pressures, were invited to see the problem the other way round – from the Government's point of view. Then, having thought about it, they were not sure whether the Government had a clear overall policy on education and training. We, the Inspectors, were hard pressed to give an answer on that point, and they in turn did not instantly come up with utopian solutions. The idealists amongst us wished we had a combined department for education and training, wondering if that would produce results. It came as a revelation to several course members to be reminded that in a number of European countries governments, whether of the left or the right, were much more actively interventionist than in this country in stimulating the economy and creating jobs. This news aroused immediate anxiety amongst some members. They feared that greater intervention by our own Government would destroy the freedom of teachers, institutions

195

and local authorities. The arguments continued in this way at all our courses. Our concern remained critical for those school leavers now dubbed as 'the unwilling, the unmotivated, the unemployed.'

Some course members said they were genuinely surprised, if not shocked, to find it was possible to discuss key issues with such frankness. One Head of Department in a school said to me, 'I can't even talk to my own school head.' Others, when put in discussion groups with a mix of educationists, remarked on the pleasure of being able to explain their own professional situations without having to adopt an organisational stance – this was over the respective roles of the secondary school and the post-16 college. Many people commented on the need to break down the barriers between school and college, and there were some inspiring examples described of joint provision, especially involving colleges with previous successful experience of providing successful link-courses for school pupils. Frequently there were course members who, both as teachers and parents, deplored the lack of guidance given to pupils in school as to the range of options available after the age of 16. Then there were the pessimists, who feared that teachers would not be persuaded to change their ways, or that they are all too insular to learn from the European experience. Other pessimists argued that teachers will find it hard to cope with classroom strategies aimed at putting students more in control of their own learning. One telling comment at one course produced howls of despair: 'I think the course has been marvellous, but unless I can have an impact on my own school when I go back, has it really been of much use?' Fortunately other course members rushed to explain how the various messages can be relayed – by careful diplomacy, written suggestions, talking with colleagues, seeking out advisers and inspectors. There was no need to organise a riot.

These insights into the traumas of school life were as much a revelation to myself as to course members. It would have been easy to conclude that unemployment, the decline of manufacturing industry, lack of respect for law and order, or whatever social factors you can think of were making formal education seem largely useless, for even graduates were not finding employment. I realised, on reflection, that while these social factors were simply making things more difficult for teachers and for pupils, there were other personal factors to be reckoned with. I remembered the words of a headteacher who had said to me in 1968, which incidentally was a year of student riots in higher education both in this country and abroad, 'Girls go into a tunnel at the age of about 14. If you're lucky, they come out of it unscathed at the age of 19.' My encounters with teachers and parents, and conversation with my own inspector colleagues throughout the 1970s, confirmed this theory. I began to feel that no matter what sort of educational curriculum you provide, you will still have to expect problems from adolescents – of both sexes, not just girls. Sooner or later, each young person will struggle to find a way forward.

Amongst several examples I knew of in the late 1970s, there was Frank, in his third year at university, doing a degree in Politics and Economics, and finding the course pointless and irrelevant, mainly because he did not think it would ensure him a job. Perhaps he lacked intellectual curiosity – or were there other problems? Frank said he was disillusioned with his former school, a public school, all male. He had found it difficult to adjust to the social side of university life and to find a girlfriend. No-one at school had ever discussed careers, merely which university he should aim for. He felt resentful of other students who claimed to know where they were going, yet he said he utterly despised any intelligent person who chose to go to a polytechnic. He felt he might take a year off after graduation, which perhaps would be of great use. At the time of this encounter Frank believed he was a victim of a system that had stifled his development and denied him the guidance he needed. He admitted he did not feel sufficiently stretched in his university course. I had no opportunity to find out more about

197

Frank's background, nor was I able to find out what became of him. I realised this was a fertile field for research, which fortunately I had not time to explore.

This was typical of the unscheduled learning I experienced on my own educational journey. I found it increasingly difficult not to respond when neighbours or friends sought my advice on matters of education. Another example, again illustrating the personality factor as much as the social factors, was Carol, the daughter of family friends. Carol's problem was not connected with rising unemployment or social unrest. Like Frank, she was a teenager in the mid to late 1970s, but unlike Frank she had passed through a grammar school, which she left with only a few modest O-levels when she was 17. She decided to become a drop-out, and much to her mother's disgust spent three years in the West Country 'bumming around', with occasional periods of employment in hotels. She returned home one day, after three years, looking a 'graduate hippy' – again to use her mother's words. Carol's mother was a nurse in a cancer hospice, and somehow managed to get Carol accepted to work there as an unqualified nursing aid. Carol had to deal with terminally ill patients, and did so for a year. Often she came home and cried from tension and exhaustion, but she never complained. Then one day she told her parents she had been accepted for full-time nurse training at another hospital. Some years later, after gaining several qualifications, she ended up as Theatre Sister in another hospital, valued for her skill and professional achievement.

These stories only served to fuel my own reservations about the educational process and to wonder if we only arrive at personal fulfilment despite our own so-called education. We glibly expect schools and colleges to be the launching pad for happy and successful journeys into adult life, when perhaps we fail as parents to see our children's real needs. It came as a profound shock to me to realise that even exalted Inspectors can fail with their own families. One colleague told me that because he was always so busy with his paper work, even when at home and supposedly off-duty, his small son, aged six, actually asked him one day, 'Daddy, can I have an appointment to see you please?' Many Inspectors, including myself, found their children were at a disadvantage at school because some teachers were unwilling, even afraid, to offer criticisms of the HMI's child. In my own case, with daughter Clare, it took me years to realise that I had no right to expect her career path should automatically take her into the realms of academe. Similarly during her childhood and adolescence, I was terribly slow to see that Clare was growing up to be her own person. Many years later, after she had walked her own trail with success, I just could not help feeling especially proud when she made her first broadcast on the BBC's World Service. I recalled the class teacher's comment on Clare's first school report, when she was not yet six years old. 'Clare is already a remarkable young orator and can hold the class spellbound with her highly imaginative stories.'

It was pleasant, like this, to remind myself that I had a personal life, yet far too often I remained permanently enslaved by work. The commitment had to go on – not just to inspecting schools and colleges but to keeping one's colleagues, especially the Department, precisely informed about the state of education nationally. Towards the end of the 1970s and into the 1980s it was still possible to feel optimistic, as we believed we were working to define the common threads that were needed in all forms of post-16 education and training. I felt fortunate to be a member of several groups that spent time discussing the knowledge and skills that people will need for adulthood and for the whole of life. My own feeling was that it is not the prerogative of particular institutions to think they have the sole solutions to educational need. Hence we had to believe that school, college, local education authority, industry, commerce, and other agencies that provide for young people must learn to co-operate and combine. Then, suddenly, when certain messages about the need for 'quality' first began to reach us, later to be followed by even more ominous ideas about 'quality control' in education, we began to realise that a new

doctrine of 'accountability' was beginning to creep in. Some-
body was assuming that educational achievement is totally
measurable, and this was to be the prelude to league tables
and other highly contentious yardsticks which would
become fashionable in the 1990s. All this was the complete
rejection of our inspectorate's traditional methods of
assessment.

Meetings and more meetings seemed to become the order
of the day, as one suddenly sensed that a more interventionist approach from on high was determining the use of our
official time. For meetings in London, for which it was usual
to go there and back in a day, my train journeys often
provided interesting interludes, even moments of light relief
on which I can still look back. I particularly remember being
on a morning train when the weather was vile and the
heating system was rather slow to respond, so I progressed
to the nearest buffet bar and obtained a carton of hot tea.
On the way back to my seat, I passed a pleasant looking
woman who smiled and said, 'Excuse me, can you tell me
where I can get one of those?' 'Well,' I replied, 'please have
this one with my compliments. I'm a great fan of yours.' I
then went back to get another carton of tea, having just met
Joyce Grenfell. On another less chilly occasion I sat next to
a retired professional footballer, whose consumption of gin
and lime was as steady as his performance had been in one
of our leading soccer teams, and that was a much more
costly encounter. Other celebrities preferred privacy, like
the former Cabinet Minister who sat throughout the whole
journey with his head encased in a monolithic pair of
headphones enabling him to listen to an audio-cassette.
Unfortunately, owing to poor technology a distorted version
of Beethoven's Fifth Symphony could be heard by all
around him. It was rather irritating, but no-one cared to
complain.

Whilst journeys on the same train as leading politicians
and other notables over the years came to be an ordinary
fact of life, it was still a rare occurrence to meet such people
officially. My one and only encounter with the then Sec-

retary of State for Education was early in the 1980s. Sir Keith Joseph had assumed his new duties with zeal and was not unwilling to get out into the battle zones of the North. On one of his forays, when he was about to open a new extension to a further education college, for which I was the General Inspector, it was part of my role to be one of the welcoming party on his arrival. Sir Keith had already put forward some controversial proposals that left certain teacher groups enraged, and the forces of unrest were relentlessly pursuing him during his public appearances. A particularly aggressive group of agitators had already closed in on the college. As soon as Sir Keith began to walk the short distance from his official car to the main entrance of the college, the welcoming party, including the college Principal, civic dignitaries, and myself, leapt forward to form a protective shield as the mob released its egg missiles and much verbal abuse. Sir Keith looked horrified. By the time we all wriggled into the college, several suits, including mine, were covered with spittle and raw egg. When I was officially introduced to Sir Keith in the calmer atmosphere of the college, he exlaimed, 'Thank God! You're one of us!' The rest of his day was made as pleasant as possible. The opening ceremony was performed without problems. At the end of the afternoon, Sir Keith escaped through a back entrance of the college and sped away with a strong posse of police.

Sir Keith at least had genuine ideas about education and was really trying to see the service in practice, whereas in the years ahead there would be many who felt his successors were more interested in photocalls and press conferences when they visited colleges. I certainly shared Sir Keith's concern about 'the bottom 40 per cent', as well as his view that teaching standards needed improvement, but in the few remaining years of my service I would be having my doubts as to whether we were really finding the right recipes for curing these ills.

12

An End in Sight

Keep right on to the end of the road . . .
Keep right on round the bend . . .

Harry Lauder and William Dillon

As the 1980s moved onwards my thoughts were turning to
retirement – no more burning the midnight oil to revise
reports, no more competing on motorways. It was like
waiting to be demobbed from the Army, but there was still
a long haul ahead of me. I would need more time to think
about 'life after HMI'. In the meantime, duty called.

Events over the years had by now convinced me that you
never know what is ahead both in your private life and in
work. Like an ostrich I had buried my head in the sand whenever the question of moving within the service had arisen. It
had traditionally been an accepted part of the system, as with
civil servants in general, that you should expect to move to
another region after a number of years. Eventually I had no
longer been able to avoid a posting away from the North-
West to West Yorkshire, with the usual domestic upheaval,
the general trauma of re-locating, and Joyce's loss of a
satisfying secretarial job in a local health centre. It seemed
that we had to grit our teeth and get on with it, whatever the
personal grief. Later on, younger colleagues would begin to
rebel against the idea of a total move for the family, and
many would live away from home during the working week
– at a price in expense, time, energy and health.

Two unexpected events added to my personal unrest as we were coming to terms with life in West Yorkshire. The first one led to the arrival at our home of two police detectives one Sunday morning in the Autumn of 1980. We had been warned that they would be calling. I invited them in, hoping the neighbours had not spotted their vehicle.

An hour later we were still in conversation. Joyce had been in another part of the house, unable to follow what was happening but getting a little curious as to why the detectives were still there. My visitors knew I had been working on both sides of the Pennines during the previous academic year. They wanted to know what places I had visited, and on what dates. They were suddenly very interested when I seemed uncertain over two particular dates. I went to fetch my work diary, which gave the answer. The detectives were at once more relaxed, perhaps even disappointed. They already knew that the diary entries could be verified by my employers. They no longer needed to talk to me, and they departed.

Their enquiries would continue. They had many more colleagues to eliminate from their list of possible suspects concerning the murder of Margot Walls. Margot, our office supervisor, had recently worked late into the evening. Walking home in the dark, she had been brutally attacked, strangled, and left dead in a suburban garden. Her body was not discovered until the following morning by a gardener. Margot had been the twelfth victim of the so-called York-shire Ripper. The police finally caught their man some weeks later. By that time the trauma of that horrific event was, especially for Margot's closest office colleagues, still undiminished. Gone was the possibility of walking alone at night. Life would never seem the same again.

A second event added to my gloom, though I should not have taken it so personally. One of the problems for Inspectors was that they had to be perfectly detached when confronted with the human predicament. In this case, which concerned the suspension of a college Principal, I had more than a passing interest since I had been visiting the college for some years and had no inkling of his sudden misfortune. I could imagine, as a former Principal, just how shocked the 'accused' must have been when suspended for alleged financial irregularities. He telephoned me privately to give me the news. Officially, as this was an internal local authority matter, and one concerning finance, it was not within the jurisdiction of myself or my colleagues to interfere. Yet I wondered what sort of private vendetta had led the governing body of the college and the education committee to take such draconian action. Those of my colleagues who knew the college and the Principal were equally concerned. None of us could believe that the charges made could be really substantiated.

The enquiry process instituted by the local authority dragged on for several months, during which time the Principal was in limbo, banned from his workplace and left to sweat. Eventually he was completely cleared of all charges. This had been a new example of the growing tensions in educational administration. It was partly to do with the tradition of the old 'town hall', whose councillors vied to get onto the education committee. Some of the 'old 'uns' would not hesitate to cut down to size the young whippersnappers running the colleges. Then you had the new-style 'corporate management', wary of the growing power of college heads as their establishments were beginning to expand into huge unilateral institutions. This was progress – gone were the old days of comfortable family-style running of colleges, with HMI as visiting uncles. Such growth, and such conflict, was beginning to make the Inspector's role even more difficult and less precise.

At this time, I was beginning to find, as did my colleagues, that our role and deployment were changing. The growth of inspectorial working groups and committees in response to Government initiatives meant greater and greater pressures for each individual Inspector. I can remember making a diagram to illustrate my own list of commitments – it contained a dozen different types of responsibility or assignment, each demanding of time and effort. We were supposed to allow agreed percentages of time for each main area of work. Most of us thought this was nonsense, especially when we remembered the days of yore when we had more freedom to plan our visits to colleges, to evaluate their work, and to give encouragement to staff and students alike. Increasingly our work programme was being centrally dictated, so that the Inspectorate was being deployed more and more to meet political pressures.

I remember once saying to a colleague that I spent as much effort wriggling out of certain work commitments as I did in carrying out others. I wanted to make a good job of a few things rather than a pig's ear out of a lot. My colleague said he did exactly the same. However, the room for manoeuvre was getting less and less, especially when the full effect of central programming was felt. This was the decision to use the whole of the Inspectorate as a unified field force, directed at targets chosen in response to the Government's current concerns. Increasingly our Inspectorial exercises were to do with courses for the young unemployed, or alternatively to gain impressions of the newer institutions trying to cater for the whole of the 16-to-19 age group. Already the arguments were under way between those who wanted to preserve A-levels as 'the gold standard' and those who felt there ought to be alternatives to suit the majority. More and more we were starting to feel like performing horses in a circus, doing what was required of us. Alternatively some saw us as Exocet missiles because of the speed with which we seemed to be descending on selected targets. It was during this decade that the Inspectorate was becoming maligned and misjudged, more than ever before in its history.

I remember, too, in my final year of service feeling overwhelmed by the number of newly introduced forms that we were being required to complete after visiting colleges to see specific courses, especially those for the unemployed. I happened to find out that there was an overworked official at one of our offices in London who had to process all these forms. He had not yet been provided with the necessary computer, and the forms as they were received were left lying in heaps. I was delighted to hear this news and decided forthwith not to submit any more of the latest returns. Nobody noticed my negligence. The system was unaffected.

Perhaps I had been an example of the shortcomings the powers that be wanted to eliminate. I longed for the days when the Inspector's work was much more informally planned and the quality of contacts with colleges was more relaxed and friendly, while still professional and helpful. I could look back on the earlier stages of my career and remember the quality of the Inspectors I had encountered both as a lecturer and a college head, and the variety of ways in which they had helped and encouraged me. It was on such a basis that I had eventually aspired to become one of them. Now it was becoming a different ball-game.

One particular inspection in which I took part illustrated many of the problems. In 1983, the Government had introduced a new scheme known as TVEI, the Technical and Vocational Educational Initiative. This was an attempt to provide courses of continuous education and training for youngsters from the age of 14 to 18, in the hope of giving them better employment prospects and also reducing the number of unemployed school leavers. Its purpose was worthy enough, but because it was hastily introduced to please the politicians of the day there was insufficient time to work it all out clearly at school and college level. The availability of new funding made it attractive to certain institutions who saw it as a means of strengthening their own position with enhanced resources, or simply getting into the education limelight.

The inspection led my colleagues to conclude that the college and the feeder schools had simply not prepared well enough for the provision they were offering. In some cases they had not really understood the kind of new approach that was demanded for four consecutive years, nor, owing to lack of time and money, had the staff been adequately prepared for their new task. On the positive side, staff and students felt a certain optimism, but this was somewhat

206

counterbalanced by the prospect of being inspected. Several members of staff already had a guarded attitude towards 'authority', and they made no bones about saying how unfair it was for a new scheme to be inspected when it was hardly off the ground.

It was also the unanimous view of all the Inspectors that this particular scheme had not succeeded in bringing the feeder schools and the college together. It was my job to produce the first draft report, and it did not meet with total approval when it went up the pipeline on our side. The problem was that relations between central Government and the local authority were already strained, and it was not thought advisable to provoke any further inflammatory reactions. I was therefore prevailed upon to revise the report, and in its final form it was suitably bland. When I subsequently visited the Chief Education Officer of the authority before the report was officially published, that was the opportunity to tell him in confidence of our real points of concern.

A root problem in all this was that our formal inspection reports were to be made public from January 1983. The matter of confidentiality between ourselves and our 'clients' was to be a thing of the past. Some would argue that this would lead to even more muted and anodyne reports than ever and that essential truths would no longer be stated. In the past HMI's conclusions had been supplied 'in confidence'. This system, in my view, had worked well, enabling in-house matters to be handled with discretion. It was only occasionally under that system that some of the more sensitive issues might have been deliberately leaked to the local or even the national press. I could not really see how such 'openness' was supposed to lead to better and more responsible evaluation and monitoring of the educational system. The Department's explanatory booklets written in 1983 for the benefit of the public explained this innovation, making it clear that inspections were intended to audit the educational system in order 'to assess the extent to which nationally, locally or in individual institutions it offers an adequate service and secures value for money.' I was not the only Inspector to think there had been, and still would be, much more to it than that.

Of course the Government of the day had been right to aim at revitalising provision for students after 16, and at reducing the number of young unemployed. Yet for me, after being concerned with the needs of young people throughout several decades, there were still some different questions to be answered, such as: Ought we to have new ways of measuring achievement, other than by traditional exams? Ought we to give better recognition to skills other than conventional academic ability? Do we use the most appropriate methods and curricula to motivate youngsters? Have we lost sight of the ideal of educating the whole man and (in these politically correct times) the whole woman?

It was fortunate that while it seemed as if the politicians would still eventually decide the fate of the Inspectorate, leading to its dismantlement, we still had opportunities within our own system to enter into debate. Inspectors were not just hatchet men, or merely clinical assessors. We liked to think, without self-delusion, that we were thinking beings, able to have an influence on educational policy, provided that notice was taken of our recommendations. So within our own ranks, as in society in general, it was natural to have a division of opinion. On one side there were those who said we must live in the real world and accept that youngsters, with the support of their parents, need to get jobs and to better themselves. On the other side there were those (I was one of them) who agreed that education has to be more than a preparation for working life. It is also about personal enjoyment – as in the experience of music, art, or gardening, or any recreation. It is about understanding ourselves, other people, and society, including technological change. It is about faith. It is about caring for others. It should be about safeguarding culture and civilisation. How can we be held 'accountable' unless we are mindful of all these questions and encourage others to think about them?

In my final two or three years of service I found myself more and more irritated not just by what was going on generally in education, but by the gradual increase of control of our work from the centre. The more astute Directors of Education and the senior staff of colleges could see that HMI's time was becoming more and more used for politically motivated enquiries. Sometimes if we had not produced the answer that was required, we would be programmed to have a second look. Where we were directed to keep on looking, only to discover huge problems, an official report would not be allowed to see the light of day, or would be greatly delayed.

I was personally concerned in two large-scale enquiries that illustrated this depressing, if not alarming, trend. The first was an exercise to report on the quality of teacher training for those in, or about to enter, the world of further education, as lecturers in various subjects. This was in response to the then Secretary of State, Sir Keith Joseph's concern about poor teaching. The upshot of the enquiry, which involved visits by Inspectors to all institutions providing teacher-training courses of this kind, was – no published report. It was not until several years after I had retired that I learned why – HMI had accurately assessed the state of play, but the powers that be had realised such great resources were really needed to improve the system that it was not possible to meet the cost, and it was best not to admit this publicly.

The other example was similar, yet more subtle. A widespread enquiry was carried out into the provision of courses for handicapped students in Further Education colleges – it would be more correct nowadays to say students with special needs. This exercise even reached the point where the first draft report was completed with unusual haste. I know this because I helped to write it, yet it was not until two or three years later that a report was published, rather low-key and not attracting much attention in the press, since by this time that particular issue was on the back burner. I happened to get a copy of the report, and eagerly dipped into it. I recognised one or two of the early paragraphs as my own writing. The rest was unlike anything from the original, and suitably bland.

Critics might say I was only annoyed out of conceit, as if I had expected to see all my own words in print. That may be true, but what was really dispiriting was the fact that money was no longer flowing into the educational coffers as it had occasionally seemed to do in earlier times. There were now even more severe arguments to justify giving value for money when money was so short. Life in general was getting more complicated and difficult, especially for the young. The educational system was supposed to be equipping them to make the transition to responsible adulthood, yet there was no certainty of employment for all. Now it seemed as if the wisdom of the older generation was not to be listened to, and all previous expectations were changing with the growth of micro-chip technology, the collapse of traditional industries, and the constant likelihood of international unrest. Given such upheaval, who would define the meaning of responsibility in adulthood?

I was preparing to end my Inspectorial service knowing I had not arrived at the answers to such questions, and sometimes wondering if I was wasting time in asking them. Yet I liked to think that I had been involved in a worthwhile task, not just swanning around consumed with self-importance. Now that we all had to be 'accountable' – HM Inspectors as well as teachers and lecturers – how could we be truly 'accountable' if we did not agree on what we really ought to be doing? Increasingly we had found ourselves at loggerheads with the politicians. They had seemed to demand instant appraisal and clever conclusions that would breed snappy, newsworthy quotes in support of their policies. Too often they had seen us, the Inspectors, as an indecisive bunch of liberals always demanding time to give matters consideration – 'trendies', 'radicals'. We were rapidly concluding, following the then Prime Minister's example, that many politicians did not want considered advice. They preferred to follow the interpretations of the press and the party faithful. Now, even within the educational system itself, there were plenty of voices criticising the Inspectorate for its bureaucratic self-interest or its fancy ideology. It was clear as my retirement arrived that it was only a matter of time before the Inspectorate would be dismantled.

There was always a negative side to work that remained unchanged over the years. It was illustrated on one of my final Inter-City train journeys, when I allowed myself to be less private than usual and was drawn into conversation with an anxious father. He was peeved when I could not offer a precise solution to his children's educational problems. He almost behaved as if I was to blame. It was not unusual, over the years, to be held responsible for all the ills of the educational system. The alternative was to be treated warily, as if you were associated with everything unpleasant that had occurred in your listener's school life. Even on social occasions the disclosure of your professional role was enough to cause anxiety. The strangest example of this reaction occurred once when I was passing through customs when returning from a holiday abroad. The officer noted the passport entry that indicated 'Government Service' against 'Occupation', and tentatively asked what branch of the service I worked in. When I told him, he exclaimed, 'Thank God, I thought you might be Inland Revenue.'

The positive side to being an Inspector had included many features. Few people had the opportunity to get such an intimate inside view of education, to be seen as the Praetorian Guard, and to influence educational practice. Perhaps the rebellion against its operation was not just a reaction from right-wing politicians but a general reaction in society against all forms of authority. I personally had never regarded myself in my work as power-mad, but others might have seen me as too authoritarian. What had mattered to me, and always will, was a desire to help others to enjoy learning, to achieve, to do justice to their families, and to fulfil themselves as God's creatures. At the beginning of my own educational journey, I had been encouraged by parents

211

and teachers, and travelled far beyond my childish expectations. Now I had reached an end, but fortunately not a complete end as other ideas began to take shape.

In my final few days, the experience of 'weeding' my office files was quite instructive. I had certainly allowed too many papers to breed, and it took many hours to vet the lot. There were some essential files to be handed on, covering current enquiries, and others to be simply binned. The problem had always been, prior to the introduction of information storage using computers, that more and more filing cabinets were needed. This would not be so within a few years' time. As I waded through the records, I began to wonder how many words I had written in 16 years of inspection – one million, two million? And what percentage would be preserved? Less than one per cent? None? Perhaps the real value was not in the written word but in the encouragement given at the right time by myself and countless colleagues to those in need – a legitimate pursuit. Most of us had served with pride. We could not believe that what we stood for was a defunct ideology.

PART 4

EXTRA TIME

The world is, of course, full of those who for one reason or another cannot face the idea of retirement ... What they want to do is what they have always done ...

1988: Robert Morley

It is not unusual for professionally employed people to feel bewildered when their employment, for one reason or another, comes to an end at some official age of retirement. One of the roads ahead is a steady path to cynicism and bewilderment as the loss of earnings and status render life less bearable. Yet many, by accident or design, find other roads that enable them to keep up their professional interests and skills, whether in conventional paid employment or working voluntarily on behalf of their local community. Eventually common sense or health factors may suggest it is time to 'retire', but many will continue, to their last, to look for a new ball-game every day for the rest of their remaining life.

As the ensuing chapters explain, I have fortunately had continuing opportunities to be actively involved in matters educational, and more recently to turn aside into more personal activities and thoughts. These in turn bring me back to education, which in this country is still failing most of its children. We are still in a right state.

For the past decade we have been told that the agenda for Britain now is the management of civilised decline. Alarmingly, there are intermittent signs that the decline is not even civilised. Naturally, the primary task of any Government of the day will be to arrest that decline, especially in economic terms. The equally important task is to create riches that are not measurable in economic terms, so that the next generation will have the real means to survive.

13

Carrying On

> If you imagine that once you have accomplished your ambitions you will have time to turn to the Way, you will discover that your ambitions never come to an end.

> *Yoshida Kenko, c. 1340*

'He's driving me mad.'

The anguished woman in front of us at the supermarket check-out was waiting for her husband, newly retired, to rejoin her – with the extra groceries he said she had forgotten.

'I've been shopping for years, and now he thinks he can tell me how to do it better.'

The two of them passed ahead, still bickering.

I had not yet shown much interest in the exercise of grocery shopping, let alone ventured to offer any opinions. I was merely acting as the patient trolley pusher, unaccustomed to the challenge of economical food purchase. It was to take me a long time to appreciate that shopping is an art and that supermarkets can show you the realities of life.

I had recently picked up some depressing messages about retirement – 'twice the husband and half the salary'. News had reached me of a nearby retired civil servant who stood looking out of the window after breakfast every morning and regularly said, 'What on earth am I going to do?' This was a highly experienced man who had spent years advising

Government ministers on the best courses of action. He eventually sorted himself out. Another fish out of water was a retired banker who, having hoped he would enjoy a permanent rest, was told by his wife to find some part-time consultancies. He did, and both of them were much happier.

All this reminded me that many people facing retirement have little opportunity to prepare for it. Perhaps it would be better if more people could gradually reduce their working week up to the final point of retirement. They would then have time to develop other interests and activities. In my own case I had year after year been totally obsessed with work, with never enough time for leisure interests such as gardening, reading, or following football. A few visits to Elland Road, the home of Leeds United, had so depressed me, because of the shabby attitude of the supporters, that I longed for the chance to return to the Old Trafford, Manchester, 'theatre of dreams', where throughout the sixties and seventies I had been a regular supporter. Joyce and I would welcome any opportunity to return to the North-West, not least to be nearer to daughter Clare who now seemed to be permanently settled there.

One thing I quickly realised was that I had not lost my interest in education, nor my concern for past colleagues. Many wrote to say how depressed they were by what was happening in education – 'even more forms to fill in', 'quirky pre-occupations and inhumane managment', 'it's getting worse'. At last, after a few weeks of feeling as if I was living in a vacuum, not having come to terms with my new freedom, I was glad to take up some further professional work – and to my delight in the North-West. For the next few years I was to have the opportunity to redevelop some of my earlier enthusiasms and to be actively involved in education again.

So before I had the chance to know what real retirement would be like, I was pleased to become involved with the English Speaking Board, with which I had been associated earlier in my career during the 1960s in the part-time role of

Vice-Chairman. I was now to have a more directorial role, working closely with Christabel Burniston, the Board's founder, in order to promote its work generally at a critical time of change, with the new GCSEs looming. The Board's approach to assessing speaking skills as a part of the whole business of personal communication had set a useful example to the educational world. ESB's spoken English examinations, preferably described as 'assessments', with emphasis on students demonstrating a variety of skill in different talking activities, had been a useful guide to the various newly emerging GCSE boards when defining their own approach to assessing oral skills. My own strong interest and belief in the importance of helping children and adults to be better communicators had burgeoned over the years. I shared with Christabel Burniston the view that education should be a total process in which all individuals must be treated as persons of potential, no matter where they have been previously placed by the educational system.

In an article in the *Times Educational Supplement*, in November 1986, I was able to acknowledge the work of the English Speaking Board during the previous 30 years in developing both pupils and teachers, as a result of Christabel Burniston's innovatory work. I also gave plenty of examples of how the Inspectorate's reports had stressed the need to make pupils and students more confident in speaking. Far too many adults remember at school being told to 'shut up' rather than to 'speak up', or being made fearful or self-conscious if asked to talk solo. The Inspectors had observed teachers talking too much for too long, and pupils proving incapable of sustained attention or fluent response. I knew the division of opinion in the Inspectorate itself between those who supported straightforward expositions by the teacher and those who favoured a more student-centred approach. Teachers were not having an easy time, since they were getting greater criticism than in the past and were being asked to meet even greater changes, with the spotlight of accountability shining ever more fiercely. Some teachers at this time were writing to the educational press to say they were tired of what was happening and could hardly wait to retire.

I was now having plenty of opportunity to sense the disenchantment of the teaching profession and the enormity of its task. If I looked back to my own years of schooling, I saw the lad with thin legs as one of many who were encouraged by parents to develop a zest for learning and the capacity to make their own healthy amusements. In contrast, while pausing from the writing of this chapter I read an article complaining that children do not know how to make up their own games, which left me wondering just what sort of children are growing up today. Nearly 40 years ago when I began teaching, television was still in its infancy, and the computer revolution had not yet arrived. Family units were more permanent, but there was plenty of uncertainty in the post-war world, and especially in education as new ideas emerged. All credit then to Christabel Burniston and the English Speaking Board for their pioneer work in demonstrating the need to make people articulate and self-confident as they progress through life.

I was glad to be associated with the work of the Board after leaving the Inspectorate and to be free to speak as an individual, not as a civil servant. At the Board's 1986 conference, I delivered a closing address that reflected several issues. I felt strongly about people's entitlement to an education that not only develops them but makes them aware of the existence and needs of others – hence the importance of the family. I spoke of the necessity to be more cost-conscious about education than ever before. I mentioned the problems of those who find satisfaction in escaping from work, and those who will never perhaps have any work to escape from. Our education system would have to become geared to a future in which some will work only part-time, many will change their occupations, and others will move intermittently in and out of work as we know it. Another decade has passed and we are no nearer to finding the answers. I did not expect that the English Speaking

220

Board had the solutions, but at least the pursuit of its well-stated aims would point the way.

Some time later, I decided to take a rest from the demands of professional work, having said goodbye to the ESB, which is still successfully promoting the importance of social competence and oral skills. Perhaps I was having a love-hate relationship with 'work,' or feeling the passage of the years. I slowly began to find how much I was enjoying greater leisure, and the opportunity to look for a more active role in the community – instead of being obsessed with work. In the meantime, I still looked forward to my weekly reading of the educational press. Then suddenly, after a chance social meeting with a senior member of a polytechnic I was invited to help with some research in the field of adult education for mature students. I was hooked, and for the next 15 months I was immersed in collecting and processing the results of a national enquiry mainly to do with the marketing of such courses.

There were several aspects of this research that particularly interested me. Marketing courses for mature students is not just a question of sticking advertisements in the press. It needs patient investigation to assess the needs of such students so that courses can be shaped to their requirements. Many of the students, as our enquiries illustrated, had left school at 16, tired of their tutelage, or not able to find enough financial support to stay on in education, either at school or at, say, a technical college, sixth-form college or college of further education. Only after some years of employment, or possibly prolonged or intermittent unemployment, do they think of doing a degree course, and even then they may have fears and doubts about their ability to cope with all the demands of becoming a student. Providers of higher education have to make allowances for these students' self-doubt, yet what many of these older students have is that quality of experience that justifies calling them 'mature'. This in turn gives them the motivation to apply themselves more successfully than they might have done when at school.

221

It was a rewarding experience to meet some Shirley and Sean Valentines first-hand, as well as processing their replies to written questionnaires. Many of them live at home and have young children, for whose care arrangements are needed. Their domestic commitments reduce the amount of time they can spend chasing around libraries. Their stretched finances limit their purchase of books, let alone of regular meals. Yet they survive, because of their determination to succeed. One student said: 'I woke up to the fact that I needed more than social security, coffee mornings, aerobics and *Eastenders* in my life.' I was also reminded that students these days, particularly mature students, are not just entering higher education in search of self-fulfilment or for a certain measure of self-indulgence. They are all part of a hard, competitive and demanding world, and they know that a professional qualification is essential. The more discerning amongst them know that the degree or diploma may be just another beginning in the search for employment.

I was lucky to have the time to reflect on my work within a research team and to pursue some of my own long-standing pre-occupations. I was aware of the contrast between my own comfortable experience of higher education 40 years ago and the more anxious, relatively serious process some students go through today. As a child, I had been encouraged to seek knowledge. As an adult, I had experienced doubts as to what the knowledge was that I was seeking, and whether the 'truth' – whatever that is – is attainable. As a teacher I had felt the urge to share my knowledge, or even my ignorance, with young people, in the hope of enabling them to find a better world or a happy life. Now it was a different ball-game for young students, for whom relaxed thinking in philosophical terms would be a luxury, if not an impossibility. Yet a certain optimism would always surface in my own thinking, especially when I had the opportunity to meet young students at their own level and to sense their energy and determination.

Any contact on my part with young students always reminded me of the basic question: what are their real needs? Students themselves, as I have suggested, are forced to take a practical view – they want qualifications, they want employment, they want a decent standard of living, they want personal fulfilment. The job of government is to provide a system of education that will meet these needs, but government also has to meet the needs of the economy. It was becoming fashionable, as well as politically arguable, to say in the 1980s that we needed an 'enterprise economy', and in 1987 this need was illustrated with the introduction in 1987 of the Enterprise in Higher Education Initiative, with Government-aided finance. For this purpose 60 institutions of higher education were selected and funded to inject elements of 'enterprise' into their degree courses but without seriously damaging the nature and purpose of the curriculum. It was assumed that the scheme would simultaneously serve the needs of students and of the economy.

I found it difficult not to have doubts about this policy. I was not alone in seeing such a Government measure as a desperate political move, a naive attempt to manipulate higher education in order to produce enterpreneurs who would boost the economy and restore our flagging national resures. It was possibly a belated version of manpower-planning, stemming from the notion that higher education can be regulated to produce the exact number of graduates to feed industry and commerce along certain pre-determined lines. Being at the coal face, as it were, of one of the establishments chosen for the scheme, I was invited to join in some of the preliminary discussions and assessments of the early stages. It was not long before I began to find some familiar problems. .

The genuine intentions behind this initiative were rather like those that had led to the Technical and Vocational Educational Initiative (TVEI) in schools. I was therefore not surprised to find that higher-education-lecturers, like school teachers, were going through the same traumas in the early stages. Institutions tend to jump onto educational band-wagons, and individual lecturers are suddenly burdened with demands they cannot yet fully understand. In a climate of financial cutbacks there is neither money nor time for the luxury of adequate staff training. I encountered individual lecturers who were bewildered by what they were being asked to undertake, or frustrated because they were not one step ahead of their equivalent leaders in other departments of the institution. It was clear to me that the real problems that go on in educational institutions are quite unknown to the outside public who so readily voice their criticisms of the system and its lack of whatever it is that they think it ought to be producing. I was finding it a salutary experience to be on the inside of the problem, but with no authority to initiate any measures that might lead to improvement.

So the basic demand remained for lecturers to introduce 'enterprise' elements as best their departments could allow. In most courses the preferred solution was to arrange work projects requiring the help of industry or commerce. This gave students an opportunity, where appropriate, to get an 'action-learning' approach. Similarly, academic assignments with a practical, work-based content seemed to be appropriate. Many of the students that I had contact with at this time were quite happy to have work-based elements introduced into their courses. In my own brief tutorial encounters with some of them, I was quite stunned by their severely practical attitude to their studies. They were not too happy to dwell on intellectual abstractions, seeking only to enhance their own idea of vocational usefulness and skill. They remain the products of their previous educational experience which has given them this false distinction between the vocational and the academic.

My short foray into the world of higher education left me with a feeling of sympathy and concern for students and staff. I was also left wondering whether I would maintain my sanity if I had to work permanently in such a demanding situation, but I found plenty of impressive evidence and hope for the future through my conversations with the heads of departments of one higher-educational institution. I recall one departmental head who said his main job is to 'reassure, smuggle, and lie to my staff that things aren't as bad as they think they are. Fortunately my colleagues are enthusiastic and collaborative.' In a second department I was told, 'We're all under pressure for new things ... the goalposts keep moving.' 'I'm piggy-in-the-middle,' said a third head. With a variety of self-images, other heads saw themselves as 'referee', 'firefighter', 'flying by the seat of my pants'. Most of the heads I spoke to were well aware of their multiple roles as entrepreneurs, systems operators, person managers, and academic practioners. The greatest role of all was to be a people manager. The list of requirements they gave me was impressive, even if they admitted they fall short in practice – 'You have to listen; to tell; to mediate; to counsel; to balance; to present the right personal image; to be persuasive; to ask questions diplomatically; to encourage; to lead – in a way that best suits yourself and at the same time helps others to give of their best.'

I did not feel altogether too pessimistic when, after this particular period of professional involvement, I decided to turn my attention to some more personal pursuits, while not abandoning my interest in matters educational.

14

Full Circle

What was silent in the father speaks in the son.

Nietzsche

'Out of the stress of doing
Into the peace of done.'

This was the inscription on my grandparents' gravestone, which was rescued from total oblivion in 1991 by Ken Lister, a kind villager in Misterton, Nottinghamshire. Mr Lister had written to say, 'No wonder you had been unable to locate the grave. The stone had long ago fallen from its pedestal and was cracked right across the middle. It was covered in nettles and undergrowth. I cleared everything away and pieced it together, leaving it lying face upward.'

No longer encumbered with the stress of continuous professional employment, I was finding time to reflect on family matters and to wonder what arduous tasks had fallen to the lot of my various ancestors, about whom I really knew very little. More than once I have been told that increased curiosity about one's forebears is a sign of old age. It was a luxury to have plenty of time at last for such a pursuit.

The cracked headstone, lying engulfed for years by nettles and weeds, symbolises the transience, if not the vanity, of most man-made memorials. While gravestones may decay, there is a permanent transfer of genes from one generation

226

to the next. A few years ago, however, that was not my immediate thought when, after a period of research, I had discovered that on one side of the family there was a long line of publicans and smugglers. From this emerged my grandfather's father, Daniel, a Church of England schoolmaster in North Norfolk, who had moved in the mid-nineteenth century to Misterton. Successive generations of teetotal Methodists had comfortably obliterated any remembrance of the early bootleggers. My own love of wine could be a matter of delayed inheritance.

My continued curiosity about family history had led me, some years after Father's death, to think more crucially about his own life and that of Mother, the values they shared, the roles they accepted, the challenges they faced. One day while browsing through my books, I chanced to dip into a school history textbook which I had inherited in my grammar school days from Father – *A Short History of England* by Cyril Ransome, published in 1907. Inscribed on the fly-leaf in his neat handwriting was my father's declaration of ownership and the date, September 1911. I had not presumed to obliterate this proof of ownership but merely to write my own name above it, with the date, March 1939. I vaguely remember in my schooldays finding its 500 fact-laden pages of small print rather off-putting. Now with different feelings I turned to the final page.

Here, encapsulated in a few sentences, was the world into which Father had been born, and a world that would change dramatically in his and subsequently in my own lifetime. 'It has been our lot,' wrote the author, 'to relate the expansion of Britain from a little island on the coast of Europe into the centre of a world-wide empire ... No other country in the world can look back upon such a long career of advancement in liberty, and at the same time of almost unbroken success as a conquering and civilising people. Let us hope that the British of the future may not be unworthy of their ancestors – a hope which every boy and girl in the country may do something to make good; and let it be truly said of us, as was truly said of some of the Roman emperors, that we have successfully united two things – Empire and Liberty.'

Father's upbringing, like mine some decades later, had rested on this secure base of belief. Service to God, King and country had been usually unquestioned. Father had gone off to war, 'the war to end wars', and had survived, unlike many other men from his village. Some years after that war, he would marry, become a civil servant, bring up a family, and serve as a lay preacher in the Methodist church for 40 years. It was only after his death, when I was sorting through his various possessions, that I gained a more personal insight into his experience of the trenches from a brief account recorded in a small notebook during his recuperation in hospital in 1918.

Towards the end of the war, he had been transferred to the 13th Yorks and Lancs Battalion, who were then on the Messines sector, which was being continuously bombarded by the Germans. 'But I survived my baptism of fire quite safely,' he wrote. 'We then moved to the Armentières front where we were continually expecting raids by the enemy, but an abundance of Flanders mud probably caused him to be content with sending "souvenirs" (including the noted whizz-bangs and Jack Johnsons).'

Some further forays up to the front line, as a member of a ration party, had necessitated exposure to German gunfire, fortunately long-range, which he and his comrades survived each time. Then in September 1918 he was unexpectedly removed from the trenches to a base hospital, because of a badly infected leg, and finally delivered to a succession of hospitals back in England to complete a slow recovery. 'There are many more musings to be written, but these experiences must be related verbally,' he concluded. I now doubt if many of these experiences were subsequently talked about. I do remember, however, during my childhood that Father was prone to headaches and was impatiently chided by Mother for being dilatory or indecisive, yet to have exaggerated those characteristics was to undervalue his sensitivity and intelligence. The experience of war had

228

impressed itself more deeply than he knew or admitted. He had endured his own set of stresses.

Just before Father died in hospital some 60 years later, Joyce and I had travelled through the night to be with him. There was a kind of impressive defiance in his smile as he said, 'You didn't expect I'd be alive, did you?' He was the quiet man, and courageous to the end. Now, as I get older, I begin to see in myself the very characteristics in him that aroused my impatience, especially his determination to make up his own mind and to be independent. That streak of independence had shown in his decision to move to a retirement home in South Lincolnshire, two years after Mother's death. He made all the arrangements before telling the family. By a cruel stroke of luck, he became victim to a virus infection soon after his move, and this particular whizz-bang finished him off. To the end of his days he had remained mentally vigorous and at least outwardly unafraid of death.

Mother, too, of course had been born into this same world, but whereas Father had been brought up in material comfort, Mother had come from a very poor family. According to an account which she wrote in her later years, she and her contemporaries were introduced to hard work at an early age. At the age of ten, having passed a school test in reading, writing, and arithmetic – known as the 'labour' examination, she was allowed to have long periods off school to work on the land, setting potatoes, weeding carrots, hoeing turnips, pulling peas, or picking potatoes according to season. 'For this, we went at 7 o'clock in the morning, with ten minutes break for a drink and snack at 10 a.m. and then dinner from 12 to 1 p.m. continuing till 4 p.m. Sometimes it was an hour's walk to the field, and the same to home, but occasionally we could get a ride in the farm cart, which was a great treat.'

For some years she lived with her grandmother, at which point 'our freedom ended, no running wild in the fields and playing by the river. Grandmother was a dressmaker, but also did plain sewing. After school I would seam long seams and overcast the inner parts of dresses etc. Grandmother worked for a farmer's wife who had five sons. All wore socks or stockings knitted by us. At eleven, I was able to knit a stocking from start to finish unaided. I didn't have much time for play. However, in the summer when she went away for a month to stay with her brother and family in Sheffield, didn't we enjoy her absence and our freedom! Yet she still left me so much knitting ... which I did during the last few days before her return. She meant well, and tried to train me to be a decent well-mannered child.'

Mother was also brought up to be a God-fearing child, through attendance at Church twice on Sunday (morning and night) and twice at Sunday school, with commitment to the Band of Hope, a temperance organisation whose weekly meetings were enlivened by the vigorous singing of hymns such as 'Jesus wants me for a sunbeam,' and 'When Mothers of Salem their children brought to Jesus'. Sad stories were delivered to the children on the subject of 'drink', and the message was reinforced with the singing of such injunctions as the following:

> 'When the drink is in, boys, all the wit is out,
> What a shame to see the men falling all about ...
> If we take the first glass, life may run to waste.
> No, no, no, we'll never, never taste.'

Despite opportunities in later years, especially on festive occasions, Mother never enjoyed alcohol. Only during bouts of illness might she be prevailed upon to swallow a little brandy, a process accompanied by the most wracked of facial expressions.

Mother was always fond of reminding us all that 'Satan finds some mischief still/ For idle hands to do,' quoting from one of those innumerable verses of Isaac Watts, the composer of 'O God, our help in ages past,' for these and similar sentiments had been ineradicably imprinted through school, Church, and Band of Hope attendance. So it was natural for

230

Mother as she grew up never to shirk any task before her, and indeed to seek employment that would supplement Father's earnings. She was a diligent worker and continued her sewing throughout her life. As a child I accepted the presence of ladies who called to be measured for whatever garments were being commissioned, and on more than one occasion, though officially removed, was able unknown to Mother to peep upon some rather voluminous feminine shapes. During the years of the 1939 to 1945 war, Mother without any hesitation committed herself to working shifts at a factory producing parachute components. At other times she worked in shops, or did voluntary work. For some time she chaired the local Townswomen's Guild, and was much loved and respected in that role. She never aspired to own or drive a car, and rode her trusty bicycle well into her late seventies, until her doctor persuaded her that angina and failing eyesight made such locomotion too hazardous.

It was my good fortune to have two such parents as role models, not that I had any awareness during childhood that parents were anything other than models of perfection, nor oddly enough do I remember any adults that set any sort of bad example to children. My own parents always cared for us and encouraged us in our own activities. Even during adolescence, but perhaps because of the seriousness and conformity of the war years, there were no traumatic confrontations. Indeed what remains foremost in my mind is the extraordinary tolerance of my parents, who were always prepared to have a serious discussion on any subject, whether it was the war itself, or human relations, or politics, a fact to which I have already referred in an earlier chapter. When they found out that I had started surreptitiously to smoke cigarettes, which I had been doing under the influence of my school friends from the age of about 13, they discussed the matter with me and agreed that if I had to smoke I should do so occasionally but at home, which is what I then happily did. Some years later, during my first few days leave during Army service, Father actually accompanied me into a local pub. I had discovered he was not averse to an occasional glass of Guinness. It was only the second time in his life he had been into a pub.

Sometimes it is not easy to sacrifice your principles to please others, but we need opportunities in life to experience different forms of togetherness and to learn from them. Our collective behaviour in a crowd, for example, may be menacing or harmless. On the occasion at Old Trafford football ground when Manchester United won the League Championship for the first time for years, I experienced the 'Mexican wave'. Across the ground in the opposite stand I saw with amusement this rapidly moving mass-fluttering of hands and bodies, and within seconds in a crescendo of noise it had travelled along to my own area, raising me upwards along with everyone else around me as we experienced incoherent delight. It happened recurrently throughout the rest of the match, each time creating an even greater, instinctive sense of obedience. Later, reflecting on this, I guessed what it must have been like to be at a Nuremberg rally, as a Hitler Youth, and to have been led in later years into various acts of barbarism. I also remembered times in my Army service when the presence of one's mates enabled physical hardship to be more tolerable because it was shared. Most of us can recall, after pleasure or pain, the joy of a common purpose achieved within a working or social unit to which we have responsibly and legitimately committed ourselves.

History can suggest that it is a matter of accident whether we find ourselves on the legitimate side of human achievement, however much we think we can determine our own ends. If I had been one of those Hitler Youths to whom I referred, I might have died as a teenager in the final years of the Second World War, a thought which came home to me forcibly 25 years after D-Day, when I had visited a German war cemetery tucked away in a village in Northern France. Each soldier had died at the age of 16 or 17. Fifty years later, in Bosnia, inter-tribal warfare has reminded us of the thin line between the civilised citizen and the savage, and the traumas imposed on a peace-keeping force. Even more recently the unexpected massacre of schoolchildren in Great Britain has led to an unprecedented level of security controls in many schools and the even more intensive vetting of the credentials of those applying for teaching posts. Politicians conveniently support campaigns for better law and order, and the increasing use of video-cameras in public places may persuade us that George Orwell's Nineteen-Eighty-four has arrived after all.

On the other hand, despite present gloom it is salutary to realise that although barbarism is a permanent factor in human affairs, civilisation as we know it still continues. Having experienced the war years, I can remember how we all felt in the early 1940s when Britain stood alone against the threat of annihilation. Yet miraculously within a few years the situation had been reversed, and that fact has always given me hope. At the same time I accept the wisdom of Sir Winston Churchill's dictum that 'eternal vigilance is the price of freedom,' and I can remember how diligently I studied the so-called 'Cold War' as it developed soon after 1945 and persisted for several decades – until, again remarkably, even miraculously some might say, the situation changed once more. It would be easy to say 'there's nothing new under the sun' or 'we've seen it all before'. Whatever the truth, there is a case for believing that if there is an unpredictable continuum of events in our history, we can influence its outcome – perhaps through religious faith, or perhaps through a striving for what Laurens Van der Post called the 'one-ness of life we are meant to share'.

If I were 50 years younger and could go back to teaching children, I would subscribe to whatever curriculum could be devised to make them have faith in the future. I cannot see why there should be so much agonising over the teaching of religious belief when all the major religions surely can be interpreted as footpaths to the same summit and to the same desire for understanding. We need to peel away much of the trappings of religious orthodoxies to get at the inner core, and to point young people in a certain direction

233

without sectarian or inter-denominational hatred. We need to liberalise, not to indoctrinate. Then on that foundation we can explain to children that because there is a negative side to the human being, we need to watch out for it. We can find it in ourselves. It can be part of our education to recognise it and to control it, often with the help of others as well as through our own religious belief. We can be ready also to confront imperfections and aberrations in others, but that is not to argue that we should be always living in a state of despair or fear. It is a matter of learning to understand people and to search for the most positive and the most enduring of human values.

When we speak of the skills to be acquired through education, especially literacy, these are not ends in themselves. They are keys to finding competence in our daily undertakings, particularly in our personal, social and working lives. The fact that children are now bombarded by broadcast images and verbal sounds of a very varied kind makes it all the more important for them to learn to be articulate. That they are less so than some of their predecessors is clear from the number of university admissions tutors who bemoan the inarticulateness of so many interviewees for higher education courses. The largely ineffective teaching of oral skills in England was constantly noted by HM Inspectors in the 1970s and 1980s, as was the absence of emphasis on speaking, questioning, and discussing in so many other subjects. This problem stemmed from the simple fact that the know-how for the development of such skills was lacking in teacher-training courses.

The consequences are apparent in so many aspects of daily life – the shop-assistant unable to respond appropriately to your request for something not in stock; the person answering your telephone call whose tone of voice instantly betrays a lack of interest; the official whose possession of an authority role has destroyed any vestige of politeness; or the participants in your social transaction who simply do not listen. These are matched by the countless men and women announcers and presenters on radio and television who either speak in a permanent flat monotone or who, in order to excite interest in a forthcoming programme, simply go sexily over the top. Are they really instructed to do this? The obsession for pizzazz now means we no longer have a simple weather forecast but a so-called weather-show. Finally, given this decline in speech standards, we now have a new variant on the intrusive 'r' (as in 'lawrand order' or 'the idearof'): the intrusive 'y' as in 'the yatmosphere'. The country now has many more 'ho-moaners' who have probably bigger mortgages than home-owners. These are, of course, petty observations. The real problem is that we have lost that sensitivity to spoken language which was once valued and encouraged. To regain and redevelop it would be the first step towards radical change in the realm of manners and morals.

Without that essential and more vigorous pursuit of linguistic competence – call it literacy, oracy, English, or what you will – there can be no truly fruitful learning, nor any eventual individual grasp of all those riches that we include in human culture. I support the former Head of Eton, Eric Anderson, who said a few years ago that we must not only speak out for civilised values but must also teach them. Macbeth, as he pointed out, is a hundred times more interesting than Mickey Mouse, and Mozart is in a different league from Michael Jackson. It is not enough, in my view, to leave people to enjoy jam butties all the time, when the pleasures of the palate can be so sensitively extended if the right opportunities can be created. I now know that I came into a career in education because I wanted others to share the joys of learning – even for its own sake, let alone for the purpose of earning a living or becoming competent individuals. Somewhere in the educational process there must be a conscious attention to getting children to know what we mean when we speak of our inheritance. If the opportunity for such enlightenment is now less and less likely to occur within the family unit, as it used to, it becomes all the more important to provide it through the process of formal education. Ideally, of course, home, school, and community should be complementary influences. Our problem as we approach the new century is that the school is expected to carry the sole burden.

At the same time I would make a plea for a little humility when it comes to the determination of curricula and learning experiences. At times when life seems more and more laden with problems, when politicians become more and more obsessive over their failure to win votes or popular acclaim, when even worthy church leaders sound as if they are losing heart, we need to look for the principles that should underlie what we attempt to teach, and we should appraise the examples we set as we teach and organise our material and human resources. For me, in that sense, the content of the curriculum is not something to be immutably defined, since the method of implementing it is more important, and the actual substance will in any case need to be changed at suitable intervals. The real test of education, the real evidence of its success or failure, will emerge only later in the lives of its recipients, by which time it will have been modified by many other personal experiences and social forces. That thought brings me back to the words of T. S. Eliot:

> ... every attempt
> Is a wholly new start, and a different kind of failure
> Because one has only learnt to get the better of words
> For the thing one no longer has to say ...
> There is only the fight to recover what has been lost
> And found and lost again and again ...

I have a very special family friend, Christopher, who in another few years time will enter that dark tunnel of adolescence through which so many teenagers have to pass. Some years ago, when he was only seven, I was with him in his own home when he suddenly said: 'People who care about people ...' It was a curious utterance, unconnected to anything that had just been said. Before I could ask him about this, he was off at great speed to his personal

236

computer, which he began to operate with ease. When I caught up with him and gently prompted his further thoughts, he replied that it was his teacher at school who had talked about 'people who care about people'. Christopher then proceeded to obliterate a line of fiercesome robots on his computer screen. Having completed that assignment with some satisfaction, he turned to me and said, 'I care about you.'

I often remember that encounter, especially on gloomy days when outwardly there is little sunlight and inwardly I recognise signs of old age. I share the optimism of all who confidently entrust the future to those we call 'the young'. My grandfather, James Juniper, who has already featured in my story, must have felt the same, when in 1928 at about my age he published a monograph on Misterton Methodism, concluding with the words:

> . . . the grandest times are before us
> And the world is yet to see
> The noblest worth of this old earth,
> In the men that are to be.'